# Home Manager

**THE ESSENTIAL MANUAL AND LOG BOOK FOR YOUR HOME**

# Your Photographs of
# Your Home

# THE ESSENTIAL MANUAL AND LOG BOOK FOR YOUR HOME

# Home Manager

*inspira*™

Quiller Press

# Dear Home Occupier

For most of us, our home represents the largest single investment we make in our lives and yet, until now, many have talked about providing a 'log book' to record all of your home details but, to the best of our knowledge, we are the first to produce it. Odd, really, that you might well have detailed information about the workings of your washing machine (if you can find the booklet that came with it!) and yet, if something goes wrong and the machine floods the kitchen or utility room, not know where your home's stopcock is to cut off the flood.

Now, with **HOME MANAGER** and your companion **HOMEFILE**, you can ensure that you and your family have a comprehensive, easy-to-use reference point for all of the important details about your home. Because it is comprehensive it will take time to complete (although you don't have to fill out all of the details at once). But think of the peace of mind and sense of control it will provide, and, ultimately, the saving of time:

- a source of immediately helpful information if problems or emergencies occur;

- a reference guide to help you ensure your home meets recommended safety and security standards;

- the means to make sound judgements and decisions regarding the purchase, sale and management of your home;

- an on-going checklist and guide for monitoring repairs and improvements;

- a comprehensive fact-file to show people if you decide to sell your property;

- one central location for everything to do with your home.

**HOME MANAGER** has been developed through extensive research and user feedback to include the widest range of relevant matters that are important to your home. We seek to improve the quality of the manual. Your comments will, therefore, be very important to us. We will be delighted to hear from you on the following:

- How might we add to or improve **HOME MANAGER** to make it easier, or more comprehensive, for you?

- Are there any aspects with which you are dissatisfied, and if so please give us your comments?

- We will be producing a CD ROM for the **HOME MANAGER** and setting up a website providing advisory services. Would that be of interest to you?

- Have you found the **HOME MANAGER** helpful and if so, in which ways?

Please send any comments to:    Building Record Limited,
c/o Quiller Press Limited,
46 Lillie Road
London, SW6 1TN

Yours faithfully,

## Home Manager

Colin Brock, Dipl Arch, RIBA, FFB, ACArch, has been engaged in the construction industry as an architect and surveyor for over thirty years. He was a board director of a major international architectural practice for eleven of those years. His experience includes the management and co-ordination of activities ranging from private housing and housing association projects to major prestigious construction projects. Associated current activity includes his being honorary secretary of the Association of Consultant Architects.

He is presently a director of Building Record Limited which operates under the registered trade mark of *Inspira*. He has received support in the development of the **HOME MANAGER** from his co-directors Michael Foote and Janusz Jankowski.

First published 1999 by
Quiller Press Ltd
46 Lillie Rd
London SW6 1TN

ISBN 1 899163 44 1

Typeset by Fakenham Photosetting Limited, Fakenham, Norfolk

Printed in Hong Kong by Colorcraft Ltd.

# Contents

# Introduction

The basic concept behind the **HOME MANAGER** and your **HOMEFILE** is that they are solely dedicated to your home. We have suggested the method by which you can set up your own filing system which we have called **HOMEFILE** throughout the **HOME MANAGER**. They stay with the home when you move on; you do not take them with you. Nearly all the details that you enter within the manual relate to your home and therefore represent essential information for the next occupier of the property. Only those particulars of a more personal nature that you will have entered in your **HOMEFILE**, and which you would not wish to pass on to the next occupier, such as your mortgage details, should be taken with you when you move.

This manual refers throughout to your **HOMEFILE**. To maintain order in your home organisation, this manual encourages you to maintain a filing structure which would contain all the matters relating to your present residence in one convenient location, your **HOMEFILE**. Most people have some form of filing arrangement yet so often we find ourselves searching all over the home, often in vain, for that elusive household equipment guarantee. When it is finally found ... it is invariably out of date. If all documents are in the one central place, your time and your money will surely be saved. You will also be preparing your documentation to be in line with Government thinking as to ways to shorten the sales process should you decide to move.

Your **HOMEFILE** can be a storage unit to suit your own particular circumstances. As an initial accompaniment to the **HOME MANAGER** it could be a very inexpensive file from your local stationery retailer. You could upgrade through time at a price to suit. We have therefore, by creating references within the appropriate part of the text of the **HOME MANAGER**, provided all that you need to set up your own version of your **HOMEFILE**. Simply create and attach a cover and dividers to your chosen container and commence the process of bringing structure and control into your home.

## BENEFITS

By helping you create a comprehensive record of the details of your property, **HOME MANAGER** and **HOMEFILE**, when completed, provide a range of valuable benefits.

- A unique record of detailed information relating to the type of property, its location, essential building features, information on public utilities and internal services such as plumbing and heating systems, electrical and gas installations. It also includes security, safety, legal and statutory data.

- The knowledge is of benefit in everyday situations and may help you and your family deal with emergencies, and in helping to deal with the home following changes within the family.

- It can help you reduce the risk of accidental damage happening to services, if you decide on home alterations or extensions.

- It will be of help if you decide to sell your property, by providing essential information to a potential purchaser.

- The records about access to public utilities may be of benefit to these and other organisations.

## YOUR QUESTIONS ANSWERED ...

Here are just some of the ways that **HOME MANAGER** can help:

**Q: How can HOME MANAGER help me if I sell my home?**

A: **HOME MANAGER** and **HOMEFILE** can give increased confidence to a buyer and may increase the speed of sale. Your **HOMEFILE** can be structured to contain all the necessary documents to meet likely Government proposals for shortening the sales process. Search documents, title deeds, survey reports, etc. can be stored in one location for passing on to the buyer. **HOME MANAGER** and **HOMEFILE** provide comprehensive information about a property.

**Q: If I find problems with my house and record them, might I not lose the sale?**

A: The Government is proposing that you as vendor become responsible for having a survey undertaken. By completing the **HOME MANAGER** you will have recognised problems at an early stage and should have taken the necessary remedial steps. Your survey should then be far less contentious than it might otherwise have been, thus allowing for a more speedy sale.

**Q: Can HOME MANAGER reduce insurance costs and claims?**

A: Yes. If all of the information about the location of mains water, electricity, gas, stopcocks and so on is completed, accidents can be minimised and emergency situations more readily dealt with.

**Q: Can HOME MANAGER help me if I decide to carry out alterations and extensions?**

A: Yes. By providing a record of existing statutory permissions, and the location of essential services that ought to be maintained or protected.

**Q: Does HOME MANAGER help owners and mortgagees?**

A: Yes. **HOMEFILE** can store all the essential documents which may become necessary to meet the Government's proposals for streamlining the sales process. Other important documents should also be retained in your **HOMEFILE**, such as household equipment guarantees, instructions for use, etc. All too often, these can get mislaid when you need them most.

**Q: How can the HOME MANAGER help in terms of maintenance generally?**

A: Operating and user instructions can be filed away for easy access. A maintenance diary is also provided, to help you organise your home on a simpler, daily basis.

**Q: Can the HOME MANAGER promote safety in the home?**

A: Undoubtedly. Helpful information about fire safety, security, hazardous substances, remedial treatments and so on, provide an easy-to-use emergency reference guide – readily available should emergencies arise.

**Q: Does HOME MANAGER promote security in the home?**

A: Yes. It encourages people to review their security and promotes peace of mind. Upgrading security may also gain a discount on insurance premiums.

**Q: Can the HOME MANAGER help the environment?**

A: Yes. HOME MANAGER contains information and data about energy conservation, thermal and sound insulation, and how to deal with such toxins as Radon gas, if you live in an area with exposure to it.

**Q: Can the HOME MANAGER promote better housing stock?**

A: Yes. It can help to increase a general awareness of our homes and how they can be reviewed and improved.

**Q: Is HOME MANAGER of value to landlords, tenants, housing associations and local councils?**

A: It is, because it provides clear information about where everything is situated, and includes information about access and means of escape, inventories and rules which apply to landlord maintenance.

**Q: How can the HOME MANAGER be more helpful?**

A: You tell us! Although the guidance notes, directories and sources of information are as comprehensive as possible, please tell us if there is room for improvement, and where.

AND FINALLY ...

This publication is not intended to provide a subjective or qualitative judgement of the individual home. Rather, the intention is to provide a means to record factual and objective answers against the data provided. The Company does not take any responsibility for any errors made by the user of this manual in the way that their information is recorded.

## How to complete your manual

The **HOME MANAGER** has been written to make the task of entering information as easy as possible and we suggest priorities for completing sections as follows:

**Complete these sections now (these are sections which are of immediate use to you as the new or present occupier)**

| | |
|---|---|
| Section Three | Utilities and Services |
| Section Four | Ownership, Tenancy, Legal and Insurance Matters |
| Section Eight | Security Review |
| Section Nine | Health and Safety |
| Section Ten | Maintenance Diary |

**Complete these sections at your leisure (these are sections which provide necessary information for people contemplating buying your home or help with improvements to it)**

| | |
|---|---|
| Section One | The Property |
| Section Two | The Environs and Local Amenities |
| Section Five | Building Permissions |
| Section Six | Construction |
| Section Seven | Finishes, Fixtures and Fittings |

If you are not presently considering placing your home on the market or carrying out improvements, then the latter sections may be left until you have more spare time. Please do not leave completing the outstanding detail until the last minute, try to pace yourself. It really is a very straightforward process for you.

**'Your Quick Response Guide'**

'Your Quick Response Guide' follows on to this section. It has been structured to ensure that essential information for you and your family may be found in one place in the event of an emergency. The guide may well help you realise that your knowledge of your home is lacking, for example that you are short on safety equipment. If so, we will feel pleased that we have helped improve your consciousness on such issues. As you progress you may well become aware of other data that needs to be recorded in the guide.

**The link between the HOME MANAGER and the HOMEFILE**

Throughout the **HOME MANAGER** there are cross references to sections within your **HOMEFILE**. These refer to the various documents which relate to the specific section of the manual and which should be stored in your **HOMEFILE**. One example would be 'Local Amenities Information', where you would store a variety of brochures and leaflets within 'The Environs and Local Amenities' section of your **HOMEFILE**. Another would be 'Electrical Test Certificates' where the certificates would be filed within the 'Utilities and Services' section.

**Setting up your HOMEFILE filing system**

You can choose any form of filing container available from your stationer whether it is a box file, lever arch file or any other style that suits your needs. Then simply add ten divider pages to record the ten sections of the **HOME MANAGER** and an index of entries for filing as cross-referenced from the text of the **HOME MANAGER**. You may wish to provide tick boxes if these documents are indeed filed away. You can also add any other entries and documents that have not been referenced in the **HOME MANAGER**.

As explained you might wish to include some pages to record miscellaneous personal contacts in addition to those contained in Section Ten of the **HOME MANAGER**.

The next heading explains how you can also include pages of details that are personal to you in your **HOMEFILE** and not in Section Two and Four of the **HOME MANAGER**. You can then remove these and take them when you move.

If you possess a large number of documents, you may need several files. In that case your ten section divider pages will be spread evenly accordingly between the appropriate files.

If you are using a lever arch file and you do not wish to punch holes in original documents such as Title Deeds, search documents, policies and certificates you can insert these in A4-size transparent plastic filing pockets obtainable from your stationer.

**The HOME MANAGER and your HOMEFILE can contain details which are personal to you**

Remember that you are building a complete picture of your home which will be of invaluable help to anyone who moves in after you. The pages in the **HOME MANAGER** which require details of local schools, churches, doctors, etc. will not be just for your benefit but will help people to move in more smoothly. You may, however, not make use of some local facilities. Your children may attend schools in another area, for example. If you would prefer not to include such personal details in the **HOME MANAGER**'s bound pages, your **HOMEFILE** can be organised to include loose sheets that may be used instead. These pages can then be removed from your **HOMEFILE** and taken away when you move on, together with all the personal documents that you have retained in the one central place, such as your will, mortgage papers and insurance policies, etc. The **HOME MANAGER** also contains a number of blank pages which will allow you to make any notes or drawings which you consider relevant.

**What you will leave behind when you move**

You will leave behind the completed **HOME MANAGER** and your **HOMEFILE** containing documents relating specifically to the property. These documents would include fitted equipment guarantees, user instructions, certificates and various other brochures and leaflets relating to your home that you will have gathered during your occupancy. At the time of this manual's publication, the Government's consultation document on home buying and selling was receiving wide attention. It is likely that as a result of the consultative process, specific documents may emerge as being legally required should you decide that the time has come to sell. These might well include a survey report, a local council search, and title deeds. Your **HOMEFILE** can accommodate any such requirements.

Good luck! . . . and enjoy learning about your home. We hope also that, when you eventually move on, you will find versions of these products waiting for you at your new residence.

# Your Quick Response Guide

Nothing is worse, when something goes wrong, than not having necessary information to hand. In cases of emergency affecting you or a member of your family, you may wish to complete the information below.

**Address:**

**Telephone No:**

**Map reference:**

**The gas isolation lever is**

**The location of the main fuse box is**

**The stopcock is at**

**Our first aid kit is situated at**

**Fire extinguisher(s) located at**

**The means of escape is**

## USEFUL ADDRESSES AND PHONE NUMBERS

In the event of an emergency requiring immediate help from the police, fire brigade or ambulance services, dial 999. Please note that this number will probably change in the future. For less critical problems the following may prove useful.

## Our local police station:

**Address:**

**Telephone No:**

## Nearest hospital with an accident and emergency unit:

**Address:**

**Telephone No:**

## Local GP/Health centre:

**Address:**

**Telephone No:**

## Emergency Telephone Numbers:

Gas: _____     Electricity: _____

Water: _____     Plumber: _____

Solicitor: _____     Tenancy/Managing Agent: _____

Insurance Contents: _____     Insurance Building: _____

Locksmith: _____     Alarm Systems Maintenance: _____

Fire Alarm Service: _____

## Other Useful Telephone Numbers:

Name: _____     No: _____

Name: _____     No: _____

Name: _____     No: _____

Name: _____     No: _____

Name: _____     No: _____

Name: _____     No: _____

Name: _____     No: _____

Name: _____     No: _____

Name: _____     No: _____

Name: _____     No: _____

Name: _____     No: _____

Name: _____     No: _____

Name: _____     No: _____

Name: _____     No: _____

Name: _____     No: _____

Name: _____     No: _____

Name: _____     No: _____

Name: _____     No: _____

Name: _____     No: _____

Name: _____     No: _____

Name: _____     No: _____

Name: _____     No: _____

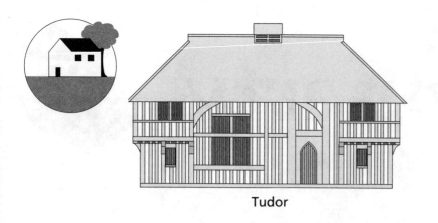

Tudor

Queen Anne

Late Georgian (1760s to early 1800s)

Early Victorian (late 1830s)

Edwardian

Late Victorian
(late 1800s to early 1900s)

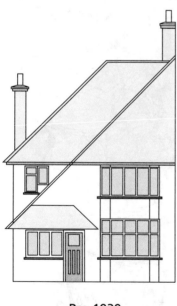

Pre-1939

Post-1939

Figure 1.1   **Periods of Construction**

2

## Section One    The Property

### ADDRESS

Postcode

If the property is in an unadopted/private road, tick here ☐

### DATE OR PERIOD OF CONSTRUCTION

*Enter the year when the property was constructed or, if not known, the approximate period: e.g. Tudor, Queen Anne, Georgian, Victorian, Edwardian, pre-1939, post-1939.*

Year ☐    ... or building period ☐

### TYPE OF PROPERTY                    *Tick ☑ boxes, as appropriate*

| | | | |
|---|---|---|---|
| *House* ☐ | Terraced ☐ | Semi-detached ☐ | Detached ☐ |
| *Bungalow* ☐ | Terraced ☐ | Semi-detached ☐ | Detached ☐ |
| *Part Building* ☐ | Maisonette ☐ | Flat/apartment ☐ | Studio ☐ |

*Other*    *(give brief description)* ☐

### AMOUNT OF SPACE                    *Tick ☑ boxes, as appropriate*

*No. of floors*          1 ☐  2 ☐  3 ☐  4 ☐  5 ☐  6 ☐

*Basement & loft*        Is there a basement/cellar? ☐  ... and/or a loft? ☐

*Floor area*             ... in square feet ☐  ... or square metres ☐

*Floor plans*            Are floor plans/room dimensions available for the home? ☐

*Recommended list of drawings useful for your home:*

Key drawings:
– Location (O.S. Sheet)
– Site Plan
Survey/record drawings:
– Measured Survey
– Condition Survey
– Structural Survey

These surveys may include:
– Ground floor/sub ground plans
– First floor plans
– Second floor/roof space plans etc
– Sections
– Elevations
– Photographs of Site/Building

The above can be provided by professionals such as architects or surveyors but if you merely wish to complete your own record of your room sizes, the graph paper at the end of this section has been provided to enable you to measure and draw your rooms to scale. This can facilitate decorations, furniture and fittings.

*Refer to DRAWINGS in* **HOMEFILE**

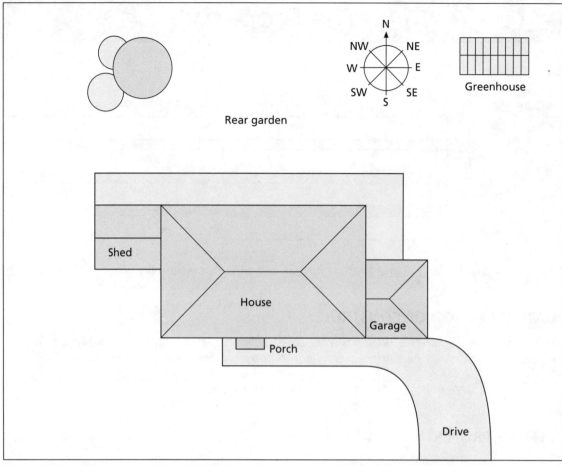

**Figure 1.2** The orientation of a south facing property with a north facing rear garden

**Position & orientation**

| POSITION & ORIENTATION | | | | | Tick ☑ boxes, as appropriate | |
|---|---|---|---|---|---|---|

*General situation*      Inland ☐      Coastal ☐      River/lakeside ☐

*Specific situation*      City or town centre ☐      Suburban ☐      Rural ☐

*Topography*      Near your home, is it:      Level? ☐      Hilly? ☐

*Orientation\**      Front of residence [＿＿＿＿]      Main garden [＿＿＿＿]

*\*Enter N (north), S (south), E (east), W (west) or points between (e.g. SE for south east, and so on).*

*Map reference*      ☐☐☐☐☐☐☐☐

In isolated or rural locations and where your home does not have a house number and/or street reference, the emergency services may recommend that you keep a National Grid Reference of the location of your property to hand. This can be passed to the services should an emergency occur. Your map reference will be defined by a two-letter grid reference, followed by a six-figure grid reference. Details of how to define your map reference are shown on your ordnance survey map. Alternatively, you can write to Ordnance Survey to obtain an explanatory leaflet.

*For the full address, see ORDNANCE SURVEY in DIRECTORY*

## ACCOMMODATION

*Tick ☑ boxes, as appropriate or quantify*

*No. of rooms*

| | | |
|---|---|---|
| Reception rooms ☐ | Kitchens ☐ | Utility rooms ☐ |
| Bedrooms ☐ | Cloakrooms ☐ | Conservatories ☐ |
| Bathrooms ☐ | . . . of which ☐ | en suite with bedrooms |
| Toilets ☐ | . . . of which ☐ | in bathrooms |

Other rooms (specify) [ ]

*Entrance*  Is the main access to the home . . . Private? ☐  . . . or Shared? ☐

## MAIN FACILITIES

*Tick ☑ boxes, as appropriate*

Does the home possess the following?

| | | |
|---|---|---|
| *Electricity* | | Electrical rewiring ☐ |
| *Heating* | | Central heating ☐ |
| *Roof* | | Overhauled/renewed roof ☐ |
| *Security* | Door entry system ☐ | Alarm system ☐ |
| *Fire safety* | Fire alarm ☐ | Smoke alarm ☐ |
| *Health* | Damp proof course ☐ | Insulation ☐ |
| | Timber treatment ☐ | Double glazing ☐ |

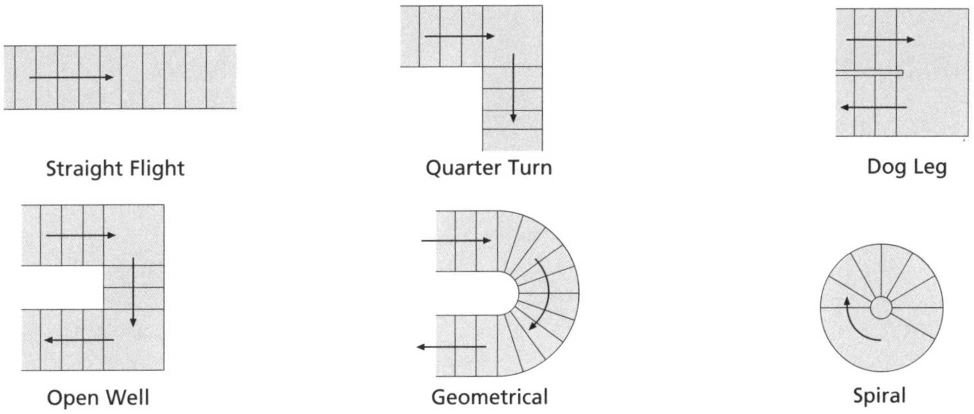

Straight Flight    Quarter Turn    Dog Leg

Open Well    Geometrical    Spiral

**Figure 1.3**  Types of staircases

## STAIRS

*Tick ☑ boxes, as appropriate*

| | | | | |
|---|---|---|---|---|
| *Situation* | Outdoor ☐ | Indoor ☐ | Sole use ☐ | Shared use ☐ |
| *Stair type* | Straight Flight ☐ | Quarter Turn ☐ | | Dog Leg ☐ |
| | Open Well ☐ | Geometrical ☐ | | Spiral ☐ |

Care should be taken when purchasing new furniture that the dimensions of your entrance door, entrance hall and staircase are adequate for access.

*Note*: A dog leg staircase rises to a half landing and then changes direction.

## ACCESS TO PROPERTY

*Tick ☑ boxes, as appropriate*

**Access to property**

*Special needs*     Access for those with limited mobility? ☐        Prams/buggies? ☐

If you are disabled you may, depending on the level of disability, require special provisions in order to gain access to the property, for example: ramps with a gradient of no more than 1 in 12, guard rails and wider front doors. Within the property you may require wider doorways, larger bathrooms/related facilities and lobbies in which to manoeuvre wheelchairs; grabrails and devices in certain rooms to assist with getting in and out of bed, washing, bathing and cooking. Reference should be made to BS 5810: 1979 Code of Practice for 'Access for the Disabled to Buildings'.

*See SPECIAL NEEDS in DIRECTORY*

*Emergency*                    Is there good access for ambulances and fire engines? ☐

Note there may be possible limitations on emergency vehicle access – for example, in a narrow street which may be further restricted by parked cars, or in an isolated rural setting where the final approach is off-road.

**Garage & parking**

## GARAGE & PARKING

*Tick ☑ boxes, as appropriate*

*Garage*                                              Single ☐          Double ☐

Integral ☐          Attached ☐     Separate block ☐

Underground car park (e.g. for blocks of flats) ☐

*Parking*          Are there restrictions?     Yellow lines ☐          Red route ☐

Are residents' parking permits available? ☐

**Outbuildings**

## OUTBUILDINGS

*Tick ☑ boxes, as appropriate*

Greenhouse ☐          Shed ☐          Boathouse ☐          Binstore ☐

**Garden**

## GARDEN

*Tick ☑ boxes, as appropriate*

*Entitlement*          Is the garden ...          Private? ☐          Communal? ☐

*Location*          Front ☐          Rear ☐          Side ☐

Roof ☐          Balcony ☐

*Features*          Driveway[1] ☐          Patio[2] ☐          Lawn ☐

Borders ☐          Trees ☐          Pond ☐

[1] Driveways may comprise tarmac, block paving, shingle/gravel.
[2] Patios or other hard landscape may comprise slabs, block paving, shingle/gravel.

*Boundary type*     Open timber fencing ☐     Closed timber ☐     Post and wire ☐

Masonry (stone, brickwork or blockwork) ☐

*Main garden Size*     Length × breadth ☐          ... or area ☐

## LEISURE FACILITIES

*Enter P (private) or C (communal) for the facilities that apply*

| | | | | | | |
|---|---|---|---|---|---|---|
| *Swimming pool* | | | Open air ☐ | | Indoor ☐ | |
| *Fitness* | Gym ☐ | | Tennis court ☐ | | Sauna ☐ | |
| | Whirlpool ☐ | | Games room ☐ | | Beach ☐ | |
| *Other* | | | | | | |

Other facilities might include shops, hairdressers, creche, laundry, clothes drying etc where they are included in residential complexes.

## HOME HISTORY

This section is purely for local and personal interest. You may wish to research or record the history of your home or local area which may include, for example, previous occupants, changes to the locality and so on.

Clues can be obtained by looking at the general style of the front face of your home for any difference with the side and rear elevations, the position of chimneys, the proportions of rooms, low ceilings, internal fittings such as doors and windows and the roof space.

Your first port of call will be your title deeds. These will list the previous occupants and may tell you when your home was built. If there is insufficient information, your local reference library may be able to assist. Your library or council should hold old electoral lists or directories which may help you with former tenant/occupier details. If these lists are not available, ask where they can be obtained.

Your county record office or your local library may also have a local history section which provides old maps and photographs of the area. These may give clues to when your home was built. Old Ordnance Survey maps and old maps in your local Land Registry Office may be available for purchase for your area from Alan Godfrey Maps.

Other sources of help might be estate agents, solicitors, banks and building societies, a local history group, perhaps, or old local newspaper archives. Long-established neighbours or elderly people living in the area may also be able to provide information which is not available elsewhere.

*The address for Alan Godfrey Maps is listed under ARCHIVE in DIRECTORY*

| *Former occupiers* | Name and any other relevant information (e.g. profession) | Date of sale or change of tenancy |
|---|---|---|
| | | |
| | | |
| | | |
| | | |
| | | |
| | | |
| | | |
| | | |
| | | |
| | | |

*Local history*

*See LOCAL HISTORY in* **HOMEFILE**

## YOUR FLOOR PLAN

YOUR FLOOR PLAN

## YOUR FLOOR PLAN

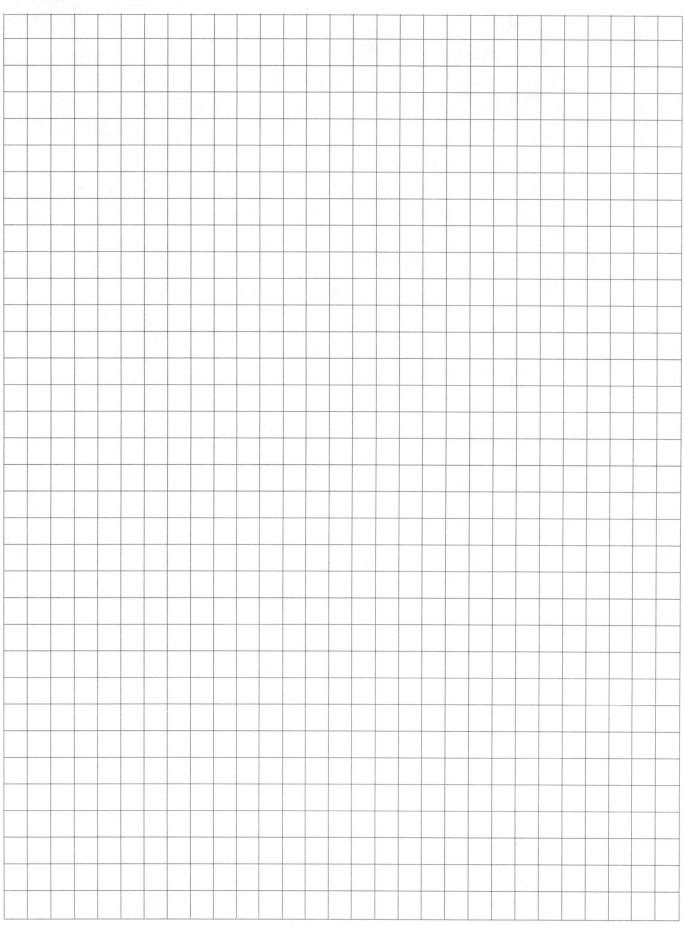

## YOUR FLOOR PLAN

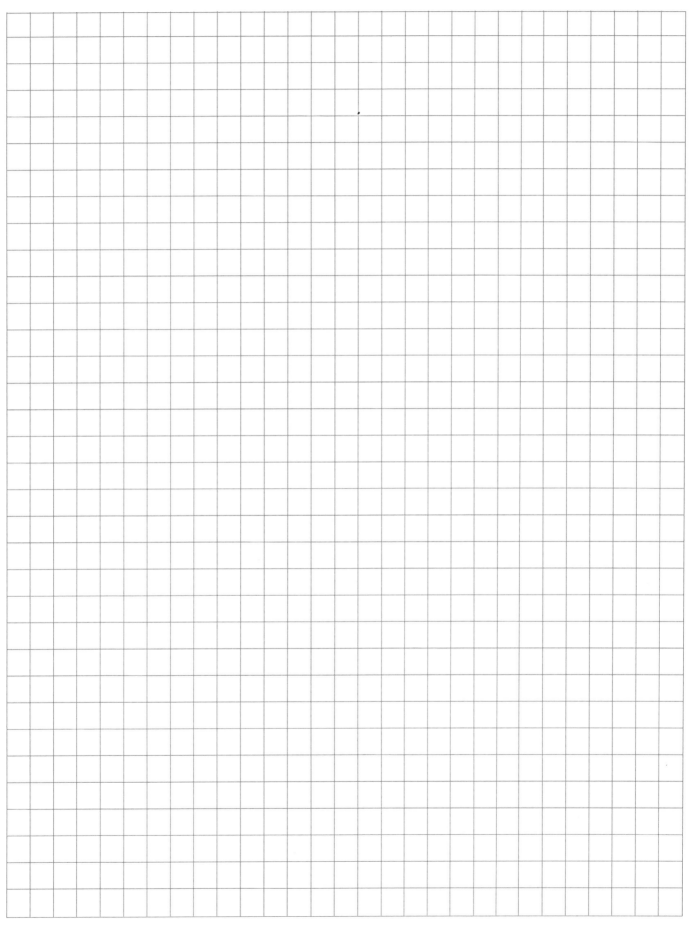

**YOUR FLOOR PLAN**

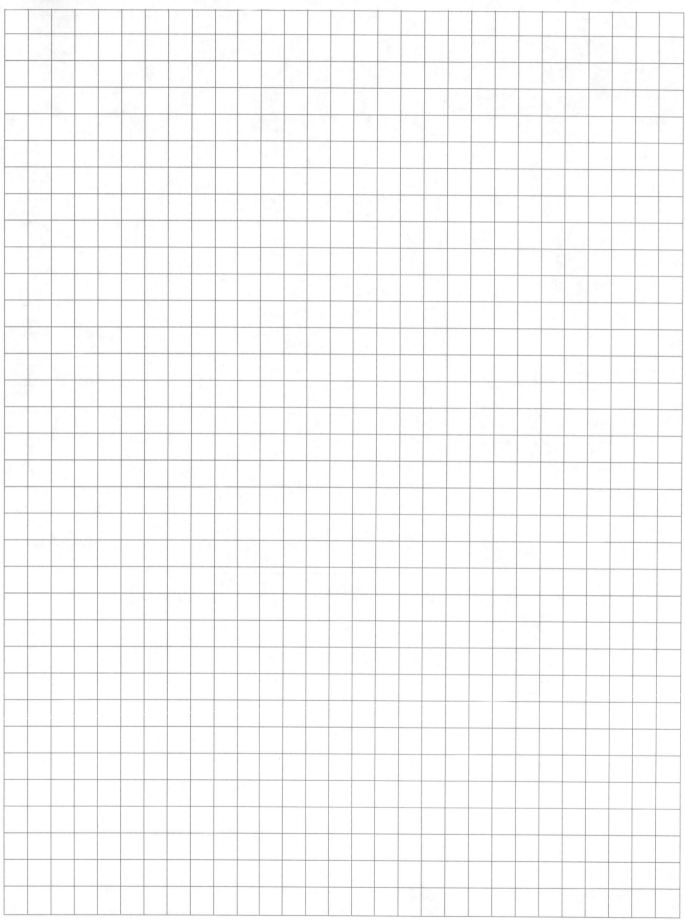

# Section 2
# The Environs and Local Amenities

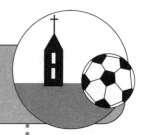

## Section Two — The Environs and Local Amenities

### IMMEDIATELY OUTSIDE YOUR HOME

**Surrounding area**   General description [                    ]

Building period [                    ]

*Description may include residential, commercial (offices, shops etc), light industrial, heavy industrial, transport, quarries, tourism (resort etc), countryside, parkland.*

**Density**   High ☐   Medium ☐   Low ☐

This refers to the density of buildings in the immediate area.

High: multistorey – for example, tower blocks or closely packed terraced housing.
Medium: flats in blocks up to five floors, or a mixture of terraced, semi-detached and detached houses less closely spaced.
Low: other housing which can include both suburban and more rural settings.

### REFUSE DISPOSAL

Refuse collection day(s) [                    ]

Location of recycling facilities [                    ]

Location of nearest public rubbish tip [                    ]

### ROAD SAFETY

*Tick ☑ boxes, as appropriate*

**Pedestrian**   Is there a pavement? ☐   Is there adequate street lighting? ☐

**Traffic flow**   Light? ☐   Moderate? ☐   Heavy? ☐

**Traffic calming**   Width restrictions? ☐   Sleeping policemen? ☐

**Other** [                    ]

### LOCAL TRAVEL SERVICES

| **Train or tube** | Station name | Minutes from home ... | |
| | | by car | on foot |
| | [        ] | [    ] | [    ] |
| | [        ] | [    ] | [    ] |
| | [        ] | [    ] | [    ] |
| **Bus** | Destination | | Route No. |
| | [        ] | [    ] | [    ] |
| | [        ] | [    ] | [    ] |

## NEAREST HOSPITAL WITH AN ACCIDENT & EMERGENCY UNIT

**Nearest hospital with an Accident & Emergency unit**

*Proximity*    Minutes from home by car [ ]    by foot [ ]

*Address* [ ]
[ ]
[ ]    Postcode [ ]

*Telephone No* [ ]    Fax No [ ]

*EMERGENCY No*    999    e-mail address [ ]

## NEAREST POLICE STATION

**Nearest police station**

*Address* [ ]
[ ]
[ ]    Postcode [ ]

*Telephone No* [ ]    Fax No [ ]

*EMERGENCY No*    999    e-mail address [ ]

## PUBLIC TELEPHONE BOX

**Public telephone box**

*Proximity*    Minutes from home by car [ ]    by foot [ ]

*Location* [ ]
[ ]

*Telephone No* [ ]

## OTHER LOCAL INFORMATION

**Other local information**

*Shops* [ ]
*Banks* [ ]
*Post Office* [ ]
*Parks* [ ]
*Sports centres* [ ]
*etc* [ ]

*See LOCAL AMENITIES INFORMATION in* **HOMEFILE**

This sub-section is generally related to the property.
You may however, wish to enter personal details
in any spare pages you provide within your HOMEFILE.

## LOCAL GP/HEALTH CENTRE

*Proximity*     Minutes from home by car [          ]     by foot [          ]

*Address*     [                                        ]

[                                        ]

[                          ]     Postcode [                ]

*Telephone No* [                      ]     Fax No [                ]

*EMERGENCY No* [                      ]     e-mail address [                ]

Local GP/Health Centre

### Emergency No:

These apply to out of hours, direct lines, caretakers, home numbers for professionals.

## LOCAL DENTIST

*Proximity*     Minutes from home by car [          ]     by foot [          ]

*Address*     [                                        ]

[                                        ]

[                          ]     Postcode [                ]

*Telephone No* [                      ]     Fax No [                ]

*EMERGENCY No* [                      ]     e-mail address [                ]

Local dentist

## OTHER CLINIC OR HEALTH PROFESSIONAL

*Type* [                      ]

*Indicate maternity, private, specialist and so on.*

*Address*     [                                        ]

[                                        ]

[                          ]     Postcode [                ]

*Telephone No* [                      ]     Fax No [                ]

*EMERGENCY No* [                      ]     e-mail address [                ]

Other clinic or health professional

This sub-section is generally related to the property.
You may however, wish to enter personal details
in any spare pages you provide within your HOMEFILE.

**Local school 1**

## LOCAL SCHOOL 1

*Indicate nursery, primary, junior, secondary as appropriate.*

*Category*

*Proximity*     Minutes from home by car [ ]          by foot [ ]

*Address*

                                          Postcode

*Telephone No*                              Fax No

*EMERGENCY No*                          e-mail address

**Local school 2**

## LOCAL SCHOOL 2

*Category*

*Proximity*     Minutes from home by car [ ]          by foot [ ]

*Address*

                                          Postcode

*Telephone No*                              Fax No

*EMERGENCY No*                          e-mail address

**Local school 3**

## LOCAL SCHOOL 3

*Category*

*Proximity*     Minutes from home by car [ ]          by foot [ ]

*Address*

                                          Postcode

*Telephone No*                              Fax No

*EMERGENCY No*                          e-mail address

This sub-section is generally related to the property.
You may however, wish to enter personal details
in any spare pages you provide within your HOMEFILE.

## OTHER SCHOOL, COLLEGE OR UNIVERSITY

*Indicate direct grant, preparatory, public, tertiary, special needs, adult/further education, denominational.*

*Category*

*Proximity*  Minutes from home by car ☐  by foot ☐

*Address*

Postcode

*Telephone No*  Fax No

*EMERGENCY No*  e-mail address

**Other school, college or university**

## PLACE OF WORSHIP 1

*Denomination*

*Proximity*  Minutes from home by car ☐  by foot ☐

*Address*

Postcode

*Telephone No*  Fax No

e-mail address

**Place of worship 1**

## PLACE OF WORSHIP 2

*Denomination*

*Proximity*  Minutes from home by car ☐  by foot ☐

*Address*

Postcode

*Telephone No*  Fax No

e-mail address

**Place of worship 2**

**This sub-section is generally related to the property.**
**You may however, wish to enter personal details**
**in any spare pages you provide within your HOMEFILE.**

**Place of worship 3**

## PLACE OF WORSHIP 3

*Denomination*

*Proximity*  Minutes from home by car  by foot

*Address*

Postcode

*Telephone No*  Fax No

e-mail address

**Other Local Amenities**

## OTHER LOCAL AMENITIES

You may enter below, if you wish, brief details of other local information eg. community centre, sports centre, pub, restaurant, theatre, cinema.

| *Name:* | | *No:* | |
|---------|--|-------|--|
| *Name:* | | *No:* | |
| *Name:* | | *No:* | |
| *Name:* | | *No:* | |
| *Name:* | | *No:* | |
| *Name:* | | *No:* | |
| *Name:* | | *No:* | |
| *Name:* | | *No:* | |
| *Name:* | | *No:* | |
| *Name:* | | *No:* | |
| *Name:* | | *No:* | |
| *Name:* | | *No:* | |
| *Name:* | | *No:* | |
| *Name:* | | *No:* | |
| *Name:* | | *No:* | |
| *Name:* | | *No:* | |
| *Name:* | | *No:* | |

# Section 3
# Utilities and Services

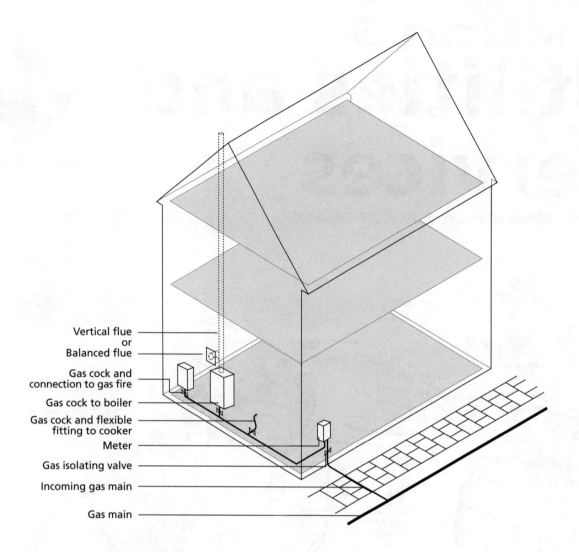

Vertical flue
or
Balanced flue

Gas cock and
connection to gas fire

Gas cock to boiler

Gas cock and flexible
fitting to cooker

Meter

Gas isolating valve

Incoming gas main

Gas main

**Figure 3.1**   Gas supply and distribution

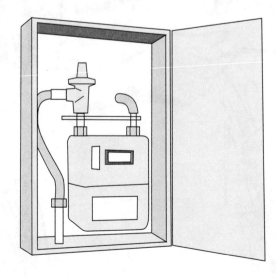

**Figure 3.2**   External gas meter cupboard used on more recent installations such as new housing, flats and conversions

## GAS

### GAS SUPPLY AND DISTRIBUTION

Gas supply and distribution

**Main**

Describe the route of the incoming gas main

[ ]

**Isolation lever**

Where is the gas isolation lever in the event of emergency?

[ ]

**Meter**

Where is the gas meter situated?

[ ]

The gas supply enters your home through a 'service pipe' which ends at the control valve by the gas meter (Figure 3.1). In most older property, meters are located internally whilst in most recently completed property, they are located within external boxes which are well vented, key operated and more easily read (Figure 3.2). If you live in a property which has been converted into flats you are advised to check with your gas supply company that your gas supply corresponds to the gas meter where readings are taken.

### Earth bonding:

It is important for the gas pipe, where it leaves the meter and enters the building, to be earth bonded by means of a green and yellow earth cable clamped to the pipe. This cable is taken back to the earth terminal on the main electricity supply. It ensures that electrical current goes safely to earth if a live wire touches the gas pipework or fittings.

### Gas escapes:

1. Extinguish all naked flames.
2. Turn off the gas at the meter.
3. Open all doors and windows.
4. Call the gas company on the emergency number.
5. Do not turn off or on any electrical switches.

### GAS SUPPLY COMPANY                    *See GAS AGREEMENT in* HOMEFILE

Gas supply company

**Name** [ ]

**Address** [ ]

[ ]

[ ]   Postcode [ ]

**Telephone No** [ ]   Fax No [ ]

**EMERGENCY No** [ ]   e-mail address [ ]

### Gas Appliances:

It is essential that gas appliances are properly vented, properly installed, regularly maintained and located in rooms with adequate ventilation in order to avoid the effects of carbon monoxide poisoning. You must by law use a contractor who is registered with the Council for Registered Gas Installers (CORGI) if you are having gas central heating installed. They will carry a current registration certificate.

*See GAS INSTALLERS in DIRECTORY*

**Gas appliances**

## GAS APPLIANCES   *See, also, HEATING SYSTEMS later in this section, if applicable*

*Boiler*                    Describe the location of the gas boiler

*Balanced flue*              Describe route to exit point of balanced flue

*Gas fire(s)*                      Where are gas fires situated?

*Ventilation*                Describe the ventilation for the gas fire(s)

*Gas cooker*                Is there a gas cooker?  Yes ☐       No ☐

**Gas boiler**

## GAS BOILER                         *Tick ☑ boxes, as appropriate*

*Model*      Name _____      Model No. _____

*Type*       Floor mounted ☐        Wall fixed ☐        Back boiler ☐

*Servicing*              Enter month of annual service _____

**Parts supplier**

## PARTS SUPPLIER

*Name* _____

*Address* _____
_____
_____      Postcode _____

*Telephone No* _____      Fax No _____

*ALTERNATIVE No* _____      e-mail address _____

## PARTS SUPPLIER

| | |
|---|---|
| *Name* | |
| *Address* | |
| | |
| | Postcode |
| *Telephone No* | Fax No |
| *ALTERNATIVE No* | e-mail address |

**Parts supplier**

## PLUMBER/GAS APPLIANCE SERVICER

| | |
|---|---|
| *Name* | |
| *Address* | |
| | |
| | Postcode |
| *Telephone No* | Fax No |
| *EMERGENCY No* | e-mail address |

**Plumber/gas appliance servicer**

*For boiler, cooker and fire connection, operating and user instructions, see details contained in the GAS AND ELECTRICAL APPLIANCE USER INSTRUCTIONS in HOMEFILE*

## ELECTRICITY

### ELECTRICITY SUPPLY AND DISTRIBUTION

*Tick ☑ boxes, as appropriate*

**Main** — Describe the route of the incoming electricity main

**Master switch** — Where is the electricity master switch in the event of emergency?

**Meter** — Where is the electricity meter situated?

**Distribution board** — Where is the electricity fuse box situated?

**Board type**    Fusewire? ☐    Trip switch? ☐

**Electricity supply and distribution**

**Electrical supply and distribution**

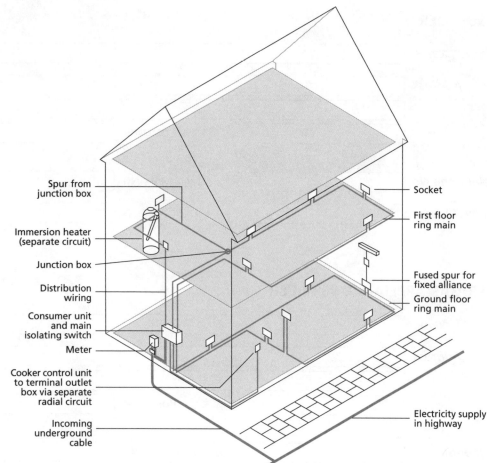

Labels on figure:
- Spur from junction box
- Immersion heater (separate circuit)
- Junction box
- Distribution wiring
- Consumer unit and main isolating switch
- Meter
- Cooker control unit to terminal outlet box via separate radial circuit
- Incoming underground cable
- Socket
- First floor ring main
- Fused spur for fixed alliance
- Ground floor ring main
- Electricity supply in highway

**Figure 3.3** A typical electrical power layout using a ring circuit. Variants include ring circuit with spurs or radial circuits.

The electricity supply enters your home through a cable leading to the electricity meter. These belong to the electricity company and must not be interfered with in any way. From beyond the meter, all cables and equipment are your responsibility. The consumer unit contains the main on/off switch and a number of fuses or circuit breakers which protect individual circuits (Figures 3.4 and 3.5).

**How to read your meter**

Although the electricity supply company take meter readings for billing purposes, you should know how to confirm readings yourself and especially if you sublet your home or have tenants. This applies to old style dial meters (i.e. non digital). Always take the last number passed by the pointer on each dial.

**Electrical safety and testing**

| ELECTRICAL SAFETY AND TESTING | Tick ☑ boxes, as appropriate |
| --- | --- |
| *Safety cut-out* | Is there a safety cut-out? ☐ |
| *Circuit labelling* | Are all circuits labelled in fuse box? ☐ |
| *Safety test* | Has existing system been safety tested? ☐ |
| *Test certificate* | Do you have a current test certificate? ☐ |

If you do not have a current test certificate, you are strongly advised to obtain one. If your home is a new property you can request one from your builder. If, at any time, you carry out rewiring, a new certificate should be issued.

Problems encountered with electrical installations can include ageing, frayed cable, faulty installation, insufficient outlets/overloaded system, wiring not earthed, inadequate fuse boxes.

The condition of the electrical installation as a whole can be checked by the Electricity Board or an approved contractor working in accordance with the 16th Edition Amendment No 2, 1997 of the Institute of Electrical Engineers (I.E.E.) regulations. Electrical Test Certificates can be provided for satisfactory existing installations, rewiring and new installations.

General Note: The route of internal electrical cables should be horizontal or vertical only to the termination points i.e. the power socket outlets or light switches. They should not be at an angle. Since these are generally concealed within plaster and other finishes rather than left on the surface, sensors can establish their location to ensure wall fixings do not penetrate cables with *serious consequences*.

*See ELECTRICAL TEST CERTIFICATES in* **HOMEFILE**

*See ELECTRICAL CONTRACTORS in* DIRECTORY

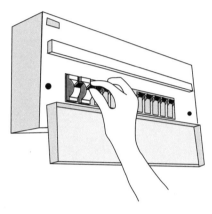

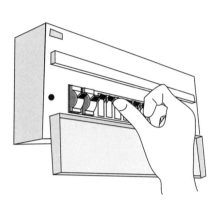

**Electrical safety and testing**

**Figure 3.4**  Distribution board/consumer unit – Remember always to switch off at the mains first before working on the electrical circuit.

**Figure 3.5**  Circuit breakers can easily be reset.

**Electrical wiring layout**

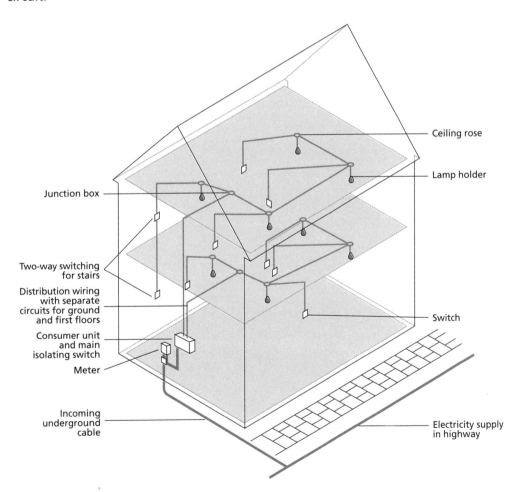

Ceiling rose

Lamp holder

Junction box

Two-way switching for stairs

Distribution wiring with separate circuits for ground and first floors

Consumer unit and main isolating switch

Meter

Switch

Incoming underground cable

Electricity supply in highway

**Figure 3.6**  A typical lighting layout using a loop-in system. A variant is a junction-box system.

**Electricity supply company**

## ELECTRICITY SUPPLY COMPANY     *See ELECTRICAL AGREEMENT in* HOMEFILE

*Name*

*Address*

Postcode

*Telephone No*     Fax No

*EMERGENCY No*     e-mail address

**Electrical installation accessories**

## ELECTRICAL INSTALLATION ACCESSORIES

*Socket outlets*     Room/Location     No:

| 1 | |
| 2 | |
| 3 | |
| 4 | |
| 5 | |
| 6 | |
| 7 | |
| 8 | |
| 9 | |
| 10 | |
| 11 | |
| 12 | |

*Special lighting*     *Tick ☑ boxes, as appropriate*

Two-way lighting switches ☐     Dimmer switches ☐

Timers on some lights ☐     Security lights ☐

Garden lights ☐

*External power*     Water proof external power socket ☐

*Swimming pool*     If there is a swimming pool, where is the fuse box? ☐

*For details of swimming pool installation, operation, maintenance and servicing, see*
*SWIMMING POOL INFORMATION in* HOMEFILE.

Electrical appliances

## ELECTRICAL APPLIANCES

*Tick ☑ boxes, as appropriate*

***Immersion heater*** Describe the location of the immersion cylinder

***Electric fire(s)*** Where are electric fires situated?

***Fridge/Freezer*** Where are fridge(s), fridge-freezer(s) or freezer(s) situated?

***Electric cooker*** Is there an electric cooker?

***Other*** Describe any other electrical items

Electricians

## ELECTRICIANS

***Name***

***Address***

Postcode

***Telephone No*** Fax No

***EMERGENCY No*** e-mail address

***Name***

***Address***

Postcode

***Telephone No*** Fax No

***EMERGENCY No*** e-mail address

*For details of electric fires, fridges, freezers, cookers and other electrical appliance operating and user instructions, see GAS AND ELECTRICAL APPLIANCE USER INSTRUCTIONS in* **HOMEFILE.**

## WATER

### WATER SUPPLY AND DISTRIBUTION

*Main*                    Describe the route of the incoming water main

_____

*Fire hydrant*            Where is the fire hydrant in the event of emergency?

_____

*Stopcock*                Location of external stopcock/access plate

_____

*Water meter*             Location of water meter

_____

*Well*                    Location of well, if applicable

_____

## Hard water and water softeners:

Hard water can cause 'furring' (narrowing) of pipes, scaling of appliances and can reduce the life and performance of fittings. Water softeners (either chemical or magnetic) can be attached to the entry points to the plumbing system to reduce these effects.

## Stopcock:

This is normally, though not always, located in the pavement or front garden, and sometimes in both. Responsibility for the pipework generally becomes that of the occupier at the boundary of the dwelling. If in doubt, contact your local Water Supply Company for any local differences. A recent development has seen the introduction of Home Service Schemes whereby some water authorities provide an annual insurance policy which covers emergency call out, repairs to fractured water pipes and clearance/repairs of blocked drains. For further information contact your local Water Supply Company.

From the stopcock, the supply pipe or 'rising main' distributes water to either a direct or indirect feed system. Most properties have an indirect feed system from the rising main to a water storage system normally in the loft. From this water is fed by gravity to the taps, WC cistern and hot water cylinder. Normally drinking water is only available from the kitchen tap which is connected directly to the rising main. In the case of the direct feed system, all cold water taps and WC are supplied from the rising main. Some direct feed systems may require a storage system to serve the hot water cylinder if one is fitted (Figures 3.7 and 3.8).

General Note: The route of pipework should avoid the same locations as electrical cables for obvious reasons. Again it should be expected to run horizontally or vertically and not at angles and will generally follow the shortest route from sanitary and kitchen fittings to serving appliances, i.e. boilers, immersion cylinders and storage tanks. This can be within casings, within the wall finish and within timber or solid floors. However, the route may be complicated by diversions/alterations that have taken place over time as the home has been altered. If in doubt contact an approved plumbing contractor before carrying out work that may disturb the plumbing installation.

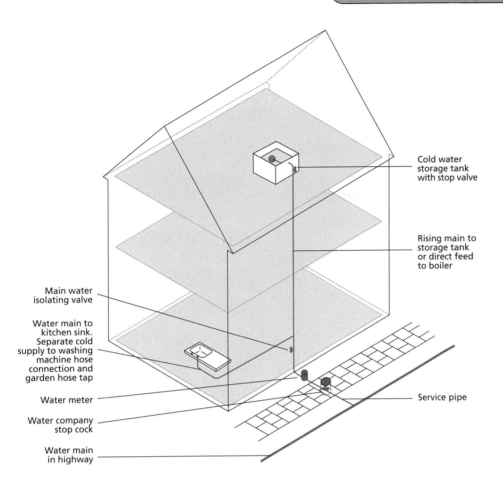

Cold water storage tank with stop valve

Rising main to storage tank or direct feed to boiler

Main water isolating valve

Water main to kitchen sink. Separate cold supply to washing machine hose connection and garden hose tap

Water meter

Water company stop cock

Water main in highway

Service pipe

**Figure 3.7** Mains water supply

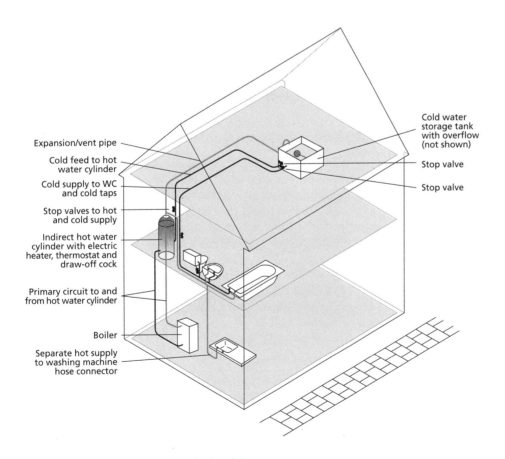

Expansion/vent pipe

Cold feed to hot water cylinder

Cold supply to WC and cold taps

Stop valves to hot and cold supply

Indirect hot water cylinder with electric heater, thermostat and draw-off cock

Primary circuit to and from hot water cylinder

Boiler

Separate hot supply to washing machine hose connector

Cold water storage tank with overflow (not shown)

Stop valve

Stop valve

**Figure 3.8** Water distribution and plumbing

**Plumbing system**

## PLUMBING SYSTEM

*Mains cold tank*          Location of mains cold water storage tank

[                                                          ]

*Expansion tank*                          Location of expansion tank

[                                                          ]

*Isolating valves*     Location of isolating valves/internal stopcocks to the following:

Cold water tank   [                                    ]

Kitchen   [                                    ]

W.C.   [                                    ]

Boiler   [                                    ]

*Do you know how to turn off your stopcocks? If not, consult your plumber or water supply company.*

*Overflows*                          Location of overflows for the following:

WC cistern   [                                    ]

Bath   [                                    ]

Bidet   [                                    ]

Wash hand basin   [                                    ]

Cold water storage tank   [                                    ]

*Drain-down valve*     Location of drain-down valve for the central heating system

[                                                          ]

*For details of sanitary and kitchen fittings, see Section Seven – FINISHES, FIXTURES AND FITTINGS.*

## Water storage cisterns, Stop valves, Drain valves:

The main cold water storage cistern and the central heating header tank which are normally located in the loft should be well insulated. Close to the cold water storage cistern is a servicing valve which can shut off water from the rising main for maintenance. Two pipes feed from the cistern, one supplies the cold water taps and WC, the other is the cold feed to the hot water storage cylinder i.e. supplying the hot water taps. Stop valves, often located in the airing cupboard, control each of these supplies and allow you to shut off the water system if there is a leak, if you need to change a washer or modify the plumbing system. In emergencies it is essential to know where these are and that they are properly labelled. Water supply pipes for the washing machine normally end with simple lever operated valves coloured blue for cold and red for hot to coordinate with the hose connections. Drain valves are normally located under the kitchen sink or near the boiler at the lowest point of the system to enable it to be emptied of water.

## Float operated valves:

These control the water level in all water cisterns. When there is a fault e.g. the valve needs adjusting, is dirty or the washer needs replacing, the water level rises within the system and drains out through the 'warning' pipe. This is located in a conspicuous position normally under the eaves in the case of the main storage cistern and central heating header tank or through the external walls for the WC cistern.

*See PLUMBING AND CENTRAL HEATING in DIRECTORY*

## WATER SUPPLY COMPANY    *See WATER CHARGE AND AGREEMENT in HOMEFILE*

*Name*

*Address*

Postcode

*Telephone No*                                    Fax No

*EMERGENCY No*                            e-mail address

Water
supply
company

## WATER CHARGES                                    *Tick ☑ boxes, as appropriate*

*Method*      How are bills calculated?      Metered ☐          Unmetered ☐

*Annual amounts*                Year                    Amount  £

                                                                                £

                                                                                £

                                                                                £

Water
charges

## WATER ACCESSORIES

*Swimming pool*          Describe the location of any swimming pool plant/machinery

*Hose supply*              Location of any external tap(s) for hose connection

*Garden sprinkler*                      Describe the garden sprinkler system

Water
accessories

**Drainage system**

# DRAINAGE

## DRAINAGE SYSTEM

*Tick ☑ boxes, as appropriate*

**Ownership**    If drainage on your land is shared with other properties, give details

 

**Connectivity**    Is the drainage system    Combined? ☐      or Separate? ☐

*Note: 'Combined' means foul and surface water*

Is drainage connected to    Main sewer? ☐    or Septic Tank? ☐

**Manhole covers**                Locations of manhole covers

**Septic tank**    Location of septic tank, if applicable, and emptying frequency

**Gullies**                     Location of rainwater gullies

Location of gullies to kitchen sinks

Soil vent pipe through roof with weathering slate and terminal

Soil stack

Rodding access door

Basin trap

Bath trap

Washing machine with trap

Sink trap

Rodding access door

Side inlet to trapped gulley

Fresh air inlet

Manhole

Interceptor

Drain to sewer

Local authority sewer

**Figure 3.9**    Foul Drainage

## DRAIN CLEARANCE COMPANY

| | |
|---|---|
| *Name* | |
| *Address* | |
| | |
| | Postcode |
| *Telephone No* | Fax No |
| *EMERGENCY No* | e-mail address |

## HEATING

## MAIN HEATING SYSTEM

*Tick ☑ boxes, as appropriate*

**Central heating**    Is central heating provided by a Full system? ☐    ... or Partial? ☐

**Heat source/fuel**    Solid fuel boiler ☐    Oil fired boiler ☐    Gas boiler ☐

Combination gas boiler ☐    Megaflo ☐    Solar panels ☐

Combined heater/storage unit ☐    Electric immersion cylinder ☐

If you do not know how to operate your boiler/heating system in emergencies or to vent air from your radiator consult your plumber.

**Location**    Location of heat source

**Heat output method**    Central heating radiator ☐    ducted warm air ☐    electric coil underfloor ☐

Off-peak electric night storage heaters ☐

**Solar heating**    If heating is by solar heating, describe the system connection and type

**Controls**    Thermostat location

Programmer location

Are radiators fitted with thermostatic controls? (Yes or No) ☐

**Radiator cleaning**    Frequency of cleaning by chemical flushing?

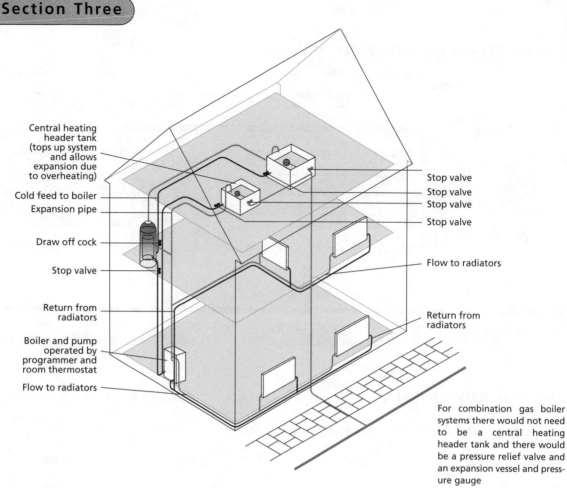

Central heating header tank (tops up system and allows expansion due to overheating)

Cold feed to boiler

Expansion pipe

Draw off cock

Stop valve

Return from radiators

Boiler and pump operated by programmer and room thermostat

Flow to radiators

Stop valve
Stop valve
Stop valve
Stop valve

Flow to radiators

Return from radiators

For combination gas boiler systems there would not need to be a central heating header tank and there would be a pressure relief valve and an expansion vessel and pressure gauge

**Figure 3.10**   A typical 'wet' central heating system

## Central Heating systems:

There are two main types:

### Wet systems

These depend on water being heated in the boiler which is fired by gas, oil or solid fuel and pumped to radiators. The radiators are normally supplied by a small header tank which should be checked annually that it contains water and that the float operated valve is working properly. This will not apply to combination boilers (Figure 3.10).

### Dry systems

These include warm air, electric under floor and electric storage heating. It is important to clean the air filter for warm air central heating units regularly in accordance with the manufacturer's instructions (Figures 3.11, 3.12 and 3.13).

## Solar heating:

The installation of solar panels can save on energy costs and over a period of time the installation cost can be recovered. The most common form of solar panel is a 'flat plate connector' usually fitted to the south facing slope of the roof and consisting of an 'absorber' plate made of a conductive material. The black surface of the conductive material absorbs light energy with water and anti-freeze solution pumped across the back of it. The absorbing plate collects this heat energy and transfers it to the hot water cylinder. A sensor automatically switches on the pump when there is a 4–5°C difference between the temperature in the collector and the water in the cylinder. A four square metre system of panels can supply 45–50 per cent of the annual hot water needs of a family with two children. There are approximately 48,000 domestic solar-powered water-heating installations in Britain.

In addition, there are 'photovoltaic panels' which provide electricity from the solar electrical panels. These are currently quite expensive but they may decrease in cost as they become more commonly used.

*See SOLAR HEATING SYSTEM USER INFORMATION in* **HOMEFILE**

*See SOLAR HEATING in* **DIRECTORY**

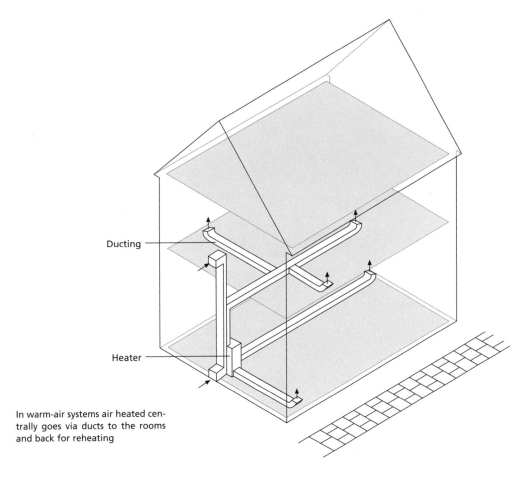

Ducting

Heater

In warm-air systems air heated centrally goes via ducts to the rooms and back for reheating

**Figure 3.11** Warm air system

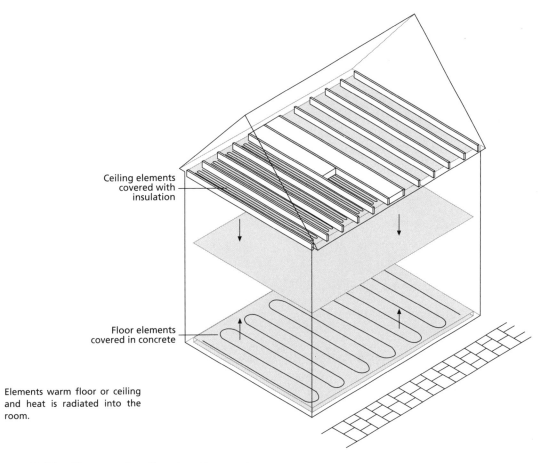

Ceiling elements covered with insulation

Floor elements covered in concrete

Elements warm floor or ceiling and heat is radiated into the room.

**Figure 3.12** Floor and ceiling heating systems

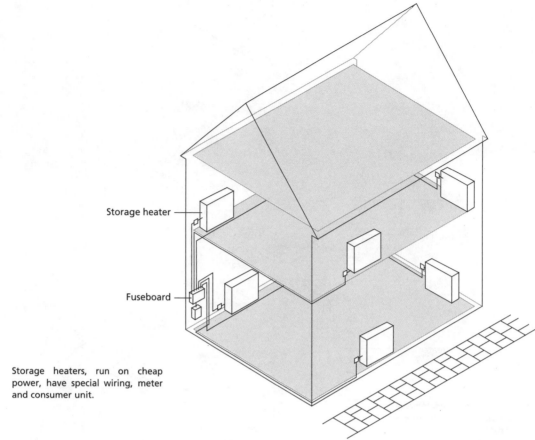

Storage heater

Fuseboard

Storage heaters, run on cheap power, have special wiring, meter and consumer unit.

**Figure 3.13**    Storage heaters

## Winter precautions:

If the home is unoccupied for more than a day or so during cold weather it is advisable to leave the central heating system on a low temperature to avoid frozen pipes.

**Secondary room heating**

| SECONDARY ROOM HEATING | | Tick ☑ boxes, as appropriate | |
|---|---|---|---|
| *Method* | Open gas fire ☐ | Gas fire enclosed with door | ☐ |
| | Open coal fire ☐ | Coal fire enclosed with door | ☐ |
| | Solid fuel stove ☐ | Built-in electric convector heater | ☐ |
| | Wood burning stove ☐ | Built-in electric radiant bar heater | ☐ |
| | Aga ☐ | Built-in electric fan heater | ☐ |

**Secondary water heating**

| SECONDARY WATER HEATING | Tick ☑ boxes, as appropriate |
|---|---|
| *Method* | Instantaneous electric water heater ☐ |
| | Electric power shower unit ☐ |

## FUEL STORAGE

**Location and Capacity**                           Location and capacity of fuel stores

**Restocking**          Oil/bottled gas/solid fuel deliveries

**Fuel storage**

## OIL OR SOLID FUEL SUPPLY COMPANY          *See FUEL DELIVERIES in* HOMEFILE

**Name**

**Address**

Postcode

**Telephone No**                                    Fax No

**EMERGENCY No**                                    e-mail address

**Oil or solid fuel supply company**

## SOLAR HEATING INSTALLATION SPECIALIST

**Name**

**Address**

Postcode

**Telephone No**                                    Fax No

**EMERGENCY No**                                    e-mail address

**Solar heating installation specialist**

## TELEPHONE, TELEVISION & COMMUNICATIONS LINKS

## TELEPHONE                          *Tick ☑ boxes, as appropriate or quantity*

*Enter in the relevant box(es) the number of telephone lines to your home. 'Regular network' means any normal telephone line from BT. 'Cable' refers to telephone lines provided by the local cable TV operator. ISDN lines are Integrated Services Digital Network lines.*

**Type**          Regular network ☐          Cable ☐          ISDN ☐

**Telephone points**          Room            No. of points

                              Room            No. of points

                              Room            No. of points

                              Room            No. of points

**Telephone**

39

## Telephone service provider

### TELEPHONE SERVICE PROVIDER

*See TELEPHONE LINE SUPPLY AGREEMENT in* HOMEFILE

*Name*

*Address*

Postcode

*Telephone No*          Fax No

*EMERGENCY No*          e-mail address

## Telephone/ accessory supplier/ servicer

### TELEPHONE/ACCESSORY SUPPLIER/SERVICER

*Name*

*Address*

Postcode

*Telephone No*          Fax No

*EMERGENCY No*          e-mail address

*For answerphone, facsimile, internet etc see TELECOMMUNICATIONS ACCESSORY USER INFORMATION in* **HOMEFILE**

## Television & radio

### TELEVISION & RADIO

*Tick ☑ boxes, as appropriate*

*TV received by*   Aerial on the roof? ☐   Satellite? ☐   Cable? ☐

Aerial in the loft? ☐

*Satellite dish*   Location of satellite dish

Location of satellite socket point

*Cable*   Location of cable entry

Location of cable TV box(es)

*Aerial*   Location of TV aerial socket points

Location of FM aerial socket points

Location of TV/FM amplifier/splitter box

## TV LICENCE

No. [          ]          Renewal date [          ]

*See TELEVISION AND FM EQUIPMENT USER INFORMATION in **HOMEFILE***

*See TELEVISION LICENCE in **HOMEFILE***

## SATELLITE OR CABLE TV SUPPLY COMPANY

**Satellite or cable TV supply company**

*Name* [                    ]

*Address* [                    ]
[                    ]
[          ]          Postcode [          ]

*Telephone No* [          ]          Fax No [          ]

*EMERGENCY No* [          ]          e-mail address [          ]

*See CABLE TELEVISION LICENCE AGREEMENT in **HOMEFILE***

*See SATELLITE TELEVISION AGREEMENT in **HOMEFILE***

## SATELLITE DISH INSTALLER

**Satellite dish installer**

*Name* [                    ]

*Address* [                    ]
[                    ]
[          ]          Postcode [          ]

*Telephone No* [          ]          Fax No [          ]

*EMERGENCY No* [          ]          e-mail address [          ]

## TELEVISION REPAIRER

**Television repairer**

*Name* [                    ]

*Address* [                    ]
[                    ]
[          ]          Postcode [          ]

*Telephone No* [          ]          Fax No [          ]

*EMERGENCY No* [          ]          e-mail address [          ]

**F.M. and T.V. aerial specialist**

## F.M. AND TV AERIAL SPECIALIST

*Name*

*Address*

Postcode

*Telephone No*          Fax No

*EMERGENCY No*          e-mail address

# Section 4
## Ownership, Tenancy, Legal and Insurance Matters

## Section Four — Ownership, Tenancy, Legal & Insurance Matters

### Cautionary Note:

The information given in this section is intended for guidance only and must be verified for accuracy and legal standing by your solicitor in the searches and enquiries that need to be made in order to obtain exchange of contracts and completion of a property transaction.

### OWNERSHIP AND TENANCY

*Tick ☑ boxes, as appropriate*

Ownership and tenancy

| Your status | Owner ☐ | Mortgagee ☐ | Freeholder ☐ |
| | Superior freeholder ☐ | Tenant ☐ | Leaseholder ☐ |
| Type of lease | Head lease ☐ | Underlease ☐ | |
| Tenancy | Previously let ☐ | Furnished ☐ | Unfurnished ☐ |

### LOCAL GOVERNMENT – COUNCIL TAX

Local government – council tax

**Borough/Council** _____

**Address** _____

_____

_____ Postcode _____

**Telephone No** _____ Fax No _____

**EMERGENCY No** _____ e-mail address _____

**Tax band** Council tax band _____

**Annual amounts**

| Year | | Amount | £ |
| Year | | Amount | £ |
| Year | | Amount | £ |
| Year | | Amount | £ |

*See COUNCIL TAX REFERENCE in* **HOMEFILE**

*Also LEGAL VENDOR SURVEY in* **HOMEFILE**

### Finding a solicitor

Consult your Citizens Advice Bureau or look through the Law Society's 'Solicitors Regional Directory' at your local library. All solicitors must have a certificate that is issued annually by the Law Society.

**Legal matters**

# LEGAL MATTERS

*If your property is affected by any of the following give details*

### Planning Office enquiries/future planning schemes

### Highway development, road widening or compulsory purchase

### Restrictive Covenants

These are usually restrictions on the use of the home for carrying out a trade or business, for the sale and drinking of alcohol, for parking caravans, for carrying out activities that may be a nuisance to neighbours and in certain areas the siting of television aerials.

### Rights of Way

### Shared rights or liabilities

This can include shared drives, sewers/drains and party walls.

### Rights of Light

### Smoke Control Orders

|  |
|  |
|  |
|  |

### Boundaries which are the responsibility of this ownership

Boundaries are often indicated in the title deeds. It is usual for the ownership and responsibility for maintenance to apply to the right hand boundary when facing the property from the front. This applies to the front and rear gardens. Sometimes the rear boundary is also applicable e.g. where it adjoins an alleyway. Party walls are a separate matter, and often need the advice of a specialist, i.e.: an architect or surveyor.

|  |
|  |
|  |
|  |

### Tree Preservation Orders

|  |
|  |
|  |
|  |

### Shared gardens – describe the form of subdivision

Where gardens are provided to flats which have been converted, sometimes divisions are along the length of the garden or across the width.

|  |
|  |
|  |
|  |

This sub-section is generally related to the property. You may however, wish to enter personal details in any spare pages you provide within your HOMEFILE. This applies to pages 48 to 51 and 54 to 56 inclusive.

## TITLE DEEDS AND SEARCH DOCUMENTS

**Title deeds and search documents**

Where the home is mortgaged the original deeds and some essential conveyancing letters and searches are usually deposited with the mortgage provider i.e. the Bank or Building Society. Where the home is wholly owned the original deeds can be deposited with a bank or solicitor in a safe or can be held in the home. Otherwise a copy could be held in the home.

Give details of the holder of the title deeds, if not the home owner

| | |
|---|---|
| *Name* | |
| *Address* | |
| | |
| | Postcode |
| *Telephone No* | Fax No |
| *EMERGENCY No* | e-mail address |

## Simplicity of purchase

Various bodies, including the Law Society, the Government and the Department of the Environment, Transport and the Regions, are calling for the home buying and selling process to be simplified. This could result in a more flexible system of mortgage lending that will allow sellers to move before their property is sold. The Government is proposing that sellers will be required to hold several key documents in a 'vendor's pack' so as to speed up the sales process.

It would mean that a draft contract, the local authority search and the basic property information is available enabling the buyer to exchange contracts as soon as a sale is agreed. Thus paperwork could be standardised and simplified and it could tackle the risk of gazumping. Private 'stockholding companies' could also buy up homes caught in a chain of sales and purchases. At the time of publication the Government has issued its consultative document. If proposals are accepted the requirements could be on the statute books in two years time.

*For essential conveyancing documentation, deeds, searches and letters, survey, see DEEDS AND SEARCHES, VENDORS SURVEY in* **HOMEFILE** *... and LAND AND TITLE and LEGAL in* **DIRECTORY**

**Insurance – buildings**

## INSURANCE – BUILDINGS

Insurance of the building covers the structure; fixtures and fittings such as baths and toilets, fitted kitchens and bedroom cupboards; interior decorations; outbuildings such as garages, greenhouses and garden sheds but not always boundary walls, fences, gates, paths, drives and swimming pools. It also provides personal injury insurance; accidental damage to underground pipes and cables; architects, surveyors and legal fees as well as the costs of clearing debris and loss of rent or the cost of alternative accommodation until your home is restored to normal.

The sum insured is based on multiplying the total metres squared or foot squared by a rate per metre squared or foot squared dependent on the factors stated below and also individual factors that can influence the rebuilding cost (*not market value*). If in doubt contact your local surveyor and/or the Association of British Insurers.

*See BUILDING INSURANCE DOCUMENTS in* **HOMEFILE**

*See ARCHITECTS AND SURVEYORS in* **DIRECTORY**

*See INSURANCE in* **DIRECTORY**

**Insurer**

**Address**

Postcode

**Telephone No**         Fax No

**EMERGENCY No**         e-mail address

**Policy number**

**Premiums**   Year          Amount £
               Year          Amount £
               Year          Amount £
               Year          Amount £

**Calculation factors**

**Floor area:**   Floor area relevant to calculations of premiums for rebuilding costs per metre squared or foot squared

**Region:**   London Boroughs and Channel Islands; South East, Scotland, North West; East Anglia, Northern, South West, Yorkshire and Humberside; East Midlands, West Midlands, Northern Ireland and Wales

**Size:**   Large, medium or small

**Type:**   Detached house, semi-detached house, detached bungalow, terraced house, flat, flat in a tenement block, mobile home

**Age:**   Pre 1920, 1920–1945, 1945–1979, 1980 to current date

**Other:**   Type of construction          Condition

Number of rooms          Number of occupants

Does an excess apply? If so, enter amount  £

*Enter number of years or percentage, as appropriate*

**Discount factors**   No claims discount          Age discount

Other (*specify*)

**Further considerations**                *Tick ☑ boxes, as appropriate*

Is your sum insured adequate i.e. to allow for total cost of rebuilding if necessary?

Have you carried out extensions or improvements that cause a review of the sum insured?

Is your sum index linked?

**Insurance – contents**

## INSURANCE – CONTENTS

Insurance of the contents of the home normally covers household goods, furniture, furnishings and all other personal items inside your home, your garage and outbuildings. It also covers spoilage of food in the freezer; loss of money, cash and credit cards; clothing; replacement of locks if your keys are stolen; valuables such as jewellery, silver and gold and specified single items; accidental damage, if selected, for all possessions at home, for mirrors and glass and for your stereo, CD player, TV, computer or video equipment. Also available, as with your buildings insurance cover, are public liability cover and accommodation expenses until your home is returned to normal.

*Insurer*

*Address*

Postcode

*Telephone No*  Fax No

*EMERGENCY No*  e-mail address

*Policy number*

*Premiums*  Year  Amount £

Year  Amount £

Year  Amount £

Year  Amount £

*Calculation factors*

Location of property in relation to premiums

*Tick ☑ boxes, as appropriate*

New for old ☐  Accidental damage ☐  Wear and tear ☐

Does an excess apply? If so, enter amount £

*Enter number of years or percentage, as appropriate*

*Discount factors*  No claims discount ☐  Age discount ☐

*Tick ☑ boxes, as appropriate*

Neighbourhood/Home Watch ☐  Physical security ☐

Burglar alarm ☐  Daytime occupancy ☐

Other (*specify*)

See *CONTENTS INSURANCE DOCUMENTS in* **HOMEFILE**

See *INSURANCE in* **DIRECTORY**

See *NEIGHBOURHOOD WATCH in* **DIRECTORY**

## EXTRA COVER

This covers personal possessions inside or outside the home and normally anywhere in the world and can include the personal possessions of members of the family who live with you personally. It also includes money, the clothes you wear, a camera, jewellery, sports equipment, bicycles and glasses.

| *Calculation factors* | *Tick ☑ boxes, as appropriate* |
|---|---|
| Unspecified items e.g. worth less than £1000 | ☐ |
| Specified items e.g. worth more than £1000 | ☐ |

New for old ☐     Wear and tear ☐     Voluntary excess £ ☐

*See EXTRA COVER INSURANCE DOCUMENTS in* **HOMEFILE**

**Extra cover**

## LEGAL EXPENSES

Do you have legal expenses protection? ☐     Legal help and advice line ☐

*See LEGAL EXPENSES INSURANCE DOCUMENTS in* **HOMEFILE**

**Legal expenses**

**Your Will**

## YOUR WILL

Your home if you own it or part-own it, your possessions, policies, investments etc. all form part of your estate. If you do not prepare a Will your property and possessions will not necessarily be disposed of as you would have wished. You are strongly advised to consult a solicitor and make your requirements precisely known. A solicitor will also advise on items of your estate that are jointly owned.

*See WILLS in* **HOMEFILE**

## If you are a Tenant ...

Registered rents attached to property can affect people trying to rent out their property under assured shorthold tenancy since the tenant can apply for a registered rent. Advice should be sought from the appropriate solicitor.

**Tenancy details – landlord**

### TENANCY DETAILS – LANDLORD

*Name*

*Address*

Postcode

*Telephone No*          Fax No

*EMERGENCY No*          e-mail address

*Tick ☑ boxes, as appropriate*

Is the property subject to fair rent? ☐

**Tenancy details – managing agent**

## TENANCY DETAILS – MANAGING AGENT

*Name*

*Address*

Postcode

*Telephone No*                    Fax No

*EMERGENCY No*              e-mail address

*See TENANCY AGREEMENT and INVENTORY in* **HOMEFILE**

## Subletting

If you are considering subletting a part of your home for additional income, e.g.: a room for a student, you may have to take into account tax payable on income received, the need to notify the Mortgage Lender and the fee charged. If you are considering subletting a whole house or flat, you should also notify the Mortgage Lender and the Managing Agent where relevant. If in any doubt, consult a solicitor.

**Maintenance and service charges**

## MAINTENANCE AND SERVICE CHARGES

This can include communal areas and gardens, entrances, stairs, lifts, corridors, roof, external walls, structure, common services e.g. central heating, hot water, lighting of the common areas, together with management costs, insurance, caretaking and maintenance.

|  |  | Maintenance |  | Service |
|---|---|---|---|---|
| Year | | Amount | Amount | £ |
| Year | | Amount | Amount | £ |
| Year | | Amount | Amount | £ |
| Year | | Amount | Amount | £ |

Details of the type and frequency of maintenance to the property, and by whom

*See MANAGING AGENTS in* **DIRECTORY**

## Purchase of council flats:

If you are purchasing a flat from a local authority, a housing association or another registered social landlord your obligations are spelt out in the lease. This sets out your obligations to the landlord and your rights. It defines the landlords obligations to maintain the building, how you have to pay for it and your responsibilities inside the flat in terms of maintenance.

If you purchase your flat under the 'Right to Buy', the 'Preserved Right to Buy' or the 'Right to Acquire' your landlord has to provide you with certain information e.g. the cost of the flat, estimates of the costs of any repairs or improvements and estimates of any service charges.

**After purchase you have the following rights:**

- to obtain a summary of the relevant costs and service charges.

- to look at any supporting documents.

- to be consulted about planned major works.

- to challenge a charge if you think it is unreasonable.

- to challenge works or services which you think are not of a reasonable standard.

*See LEASEHOLD/RIGHT TO BUY in DIRECTORY*

## House purchase/mortgages:

If you are trying to find out details of a mortgage lender this can be obtained from the 'Directory of Members' produced by the Council of Mortgage Lenders.

They can also send you leaflets which set out the tax rules governing mortgage interest and which explain mortgage indemnity.

The Office of Fair Trading produces a leaflet on personal finance which gives guidance on the different types of mortgage repayment methods and the factors affecting the choice of mortgage. They also publish a leaflet on estate agency which explains the process of buying and selling a property and advises on contracts, charges, selling rights, making an offer, repossessed property, gazumping, deposits, valuations and legal matters.

If you are self employed or have been turned down at a bank or building society or have a problem with your credit rating, you may wish to obtain a mortgage through a mortgage broker. The Mortgage Code is a self regulating code of practice which guarantees you fair advice and a right to complain if something goes wrong.

*See MORTGAGES in DIRECTORY*

## Methods of purchase of your home. The options:

Apart from outright payment, the use of a bank loan, or a mortgage obtained from a building society or bank, there are other methods of home purchase. There are Government schemes which can help you buy your own home at a price you can afford.

- Buy through the traditional mortgage route.

- Buy your council or housing association home at a discount under the Right to Buy scheme or the Rent to Mortgage scheme.

- Buy an empty home at a discount through the Voluntary Sales scheme.

- Obtain a cash boost to buy on the open market through the Cash Incentive schemes and Tenants Incentive schemes.

- Buy a share of a home through the Shared Ownership scheme.

- Buy an older home that has been improved under the Improvement for Sale scheme.

- Buy an older home and improve it yourself under the Homesteading scheme.

- Buy a warden-assisted flat or bungalow under the Leasehold for the Elderly scheme.

- Obtain help, and build your own home under the Self Build scheme.

**Further Information**

Further information can be obtained by reference to the booklet, 'How to buy a home', produced by the Council of Mortgage Lenders. There are also reference leaflets produced by the individual Building Societies.

Ask at the Town Hall or local housing advice centre, your housing association or the regional office of the Housing Corporation as appropriate. The free booklet, 'Your Right to Buy Your Home' is available from your local council or from the Department of the Environment, Transport and the Regions.

The Leasehold Reform, Housing and Urban Development Act 1993 amended certain rights, which apply to leaseholders of flats in relation to buying the freehold, or extending or renewing the lease

and the right to a management audit. The 1967 Act conferred the right to certain leaseholders of houses to purchase the freehold or to extend the lease. The Housing Act 1996 has amended both these acts in certain respects.

It is advisable to get detailed advice from professional people, such as lawyers, qualified surveyors or incorporated valuers.

*See EMPTY HOMES in DIRECTORY*

*See FINANCE in DIRECTORY*

*See HOME PURCHASE in DIRECTORY*

*See HOUSING ASSOCIATIONS in DIRECTORY*

*See LEASEHOLD/RIGHT TO BUY in DIRECTORY*

*See SELF BUILD in DIRECTORY*

*See VALUATION AND RENT ASSESSMENT in DIRECTORY*

## If you have a Mortgage and Policies . . .

**Mortgage provider**

### MORTGAGE PROVIDER

Company Name _____

Address _____

Postcode _____

Telephone No _____     Fax No _____

EMERGENCY No _____     e-mail address _____

Roll Number _____

**Mortgage details**

### MORTGAGE DETAILS     *Tick ☑ boxes, as appropriate*

Purchase details     Price £ _____     Date _____

Mortgage     Amount £ _____     Commenced _____

Duration of mortgage, in years ___

Mortgage type     Repayment ☐     Endowment ☐     Pension linked ☐

Eurotrust investment linked ☐     PEP linked ☐     Other ☐

Amount

Current balance     Date ___     Capital £ ___

Interest £ ___

Date ___     Capital £ ___

Interest £ ___

## POLICY PROVIDER 1

*Company name*

*Address*

Postcode

*Telephone No*

Fax No

*EMERGENCY No*

e-mail address

*Policy Number*

Policy provider 1

## POLICY PROVIDER 2

*Company name*

*Address*

Postcode

*Telephone No*

Fax No

*EMERGENCY No*

e-mail address

*Policy Number*

Policy provider 2

## MORTGAGE GUARANTEE POLICY PROVIDER

This guarantee policy is taken out to guarantee payment of the mortgage in case of death and acts as a life assurance.

*Company name*

*Address*

Postcode

*Telephone No*

Fax No

*EMERGENCY No*

e-mail address

*Policy Number*

Mortgage guarantee policy provider

**Mortgage repayment protection provider**

## MORTGAGE REPAYMENT PROTECTION PROVIDER

This protection policy protects payment of the premiums for a limited period and may cover sickness, accident and redundancy. It comes into effect after a set waiting period.

*Company name*

*Address*

Postcode

*Telephone No*      Fax No

*EMERGENCY No*      e-mail address

*Policy Number*

*See MORTGAGE AND POLICY DOCUMENTS in* **HOMEFILE**

**Notes**

**MODIFICATIONS TO THE PROPERTY**

*Tick ☑ boxes, as appropriate*

*Is your home ...*

Purpose-built? ☐    Converted? ☐

Describe any alterations or extensions.

☐

☐

## PLANNING PERMISSION

Most alterations and external changes to your home require planning permission but many works are covered by an automatic planning permission which is known as permitted development. Loft conversions which extend beyond the plane of the roof, work in conservation areas and material changes to the front elevation facing the street will require planning permission. Drop kerbs to allow car access sometimes require planning permission if giving access to a major highway, as do alterations to some garden walls and the installation of a satellite dish in certain circumstances. These are covered by the Town and Country Planning (General Permitted Development) Order S.I. 1995 No 418.

### Full planning application:

This is a means of establishing whether an alteration is likely to be permitted and requires information on the type of building materials, colours and finishes to be used as well as layout and elevations. It can also establish whether a property is allowed a change of use, e.g: commercial property converted to residential. Planning permission is automatically required for alterations to flats and maisonettes.

Note: Outline Planning applications are very rare for domestic alterations and are normally discouraged in favour of making a full planning application.

*Tick ☑ boxes, as appropriate*

*Full applications*  Approved ☐  Rejected ☐

Application date ☐    Last date approved/rejected ☐

Application reference number ☐

Enter conditions attached to approval, or reason for refusal

☐

☐

☐

☐

☐

☐

☐

☐

☐

## CHANGE OF USE

**Change of use**

If property is used partly for business or as an office, this can mean loss of MIRAS tax relief, and can lead to capital gains tax on the sale of the property. It can also necessitate special insurance being required for equipment used for carrying out an occupation. Planning permission will be required for use of a residence as a business if the residence does not remain mainly a private residence, if it causes a rise in traffic or people calling, if it disturbs neighbours at unreasonable hours, if it creates a nuisance such as noise or smells, and if it involves any activities unusual in a residential area.

*Tick ☑ boxes, as appropriate*

Has change of use been applied for? ☐     Is property used partly for business? ☐

**Subdivision**

## SUBDIVISION

This can include provision of a separate self contained flat, granny annex, etc. If a property is sub-divided, is in multiple occupation (more than six people) and is changed to form two or more flats, planning permission will be required.

*Tick ☑ boxes, as appropriate*

Is the property self-contained? ☐     ... or under separate use? ☐

**Other planning matters**

## OTHER PLANNING MATTERS

### Conservation Areas

These consist of a collection of buildings/streets comprising housing and other buildings of merit where restrictions apply on the form and size of extensions and on the use of replacement materials including doors and windows. An application must be submitted for conservation area consent in order to carry out work to a building in a conservation area. Information should be obtained from your local planning department.

Name of conservation area ☐

Details of any restrictions

☐
☐
☐

*Tick ☑ boxes, as appropriate*

Conservation Area Consent ...     Approved ☐     Refused ☐

Application date ☐     Last date approved/rejected ☐

Application reference number ☐

Enter conditions attached to approval, or reason for refusal

☐
☐
☐

## Listed Buildings

These are buildings of historic importance/architectural merit. More stringent restrictions apply. An application must be submitted for listed building consent in order to carry out any work to a listed building. Information should be obtained from your local planning department and the Department of Environment, or from English Heritage.

Historic buildings are entered on the list by the Department of National Heritage. You should contact them *only* if you wish to try to remove your building from the list.

Grade of listing where applicable [＿＿＿＿]

Enter Details

[＿＿＿＿＿＿＿＿＿＿＿＿＿＿]
[＿＿＿＿＿＿＿＿＿＿＿＿＿＿]
[＿＿＿＿＿＿＿＿＿＿＿＿＿＿]

*Tick ☑ boxes, as appropriate*

Listed Building Consent . . .     Approved [ ]     Refused [ ]

Application date [＿｜＿]     Last date approved/rejected [＿｜＿]

Application reference number [＿＿＿＿]

Enter conditions attached to approval, or reason for refusal

[＿＿＿＿＿＿＿＿＿＿＿＿]
[＿＿＿＿＿＿＿＿＿＿＿＿]
[＿＿＿＿＿＿＿＿＿＿＿＿]

### Historical buildings at risk:

English Heritage has carried out the first national audit of England's outstanding historic buildings at risk through neglect and decay. Of the 28,000 Grade I and II buildings, in excess of 1,500 need urgent repair. 'The English Heritage Register of Buildings at Risk 1998' provides practical guidance, advice and grants to local authorities, building preservation trusts, owners and members of the public who are in a position to save a building at risk. English Heritage has also launched 'A New Strategy' which makes available a sum of money, defines the actions required and makes available five new grant schemes.

*See HISTORIC BUILDINGS in DIRECTORY*

## Tree Preservation Orders

Before trees in conservation areas can be removed, or pruned to an agreed amount, six weeks' notice is required and an application needs to be submitted by an approved agent, tree surgeon, or landscape maintenance company.

*Tick ☑ boxes, as appropriate*

Is the property within a conservation area, subject to tree preservation orders? [ ]

Date permission obtained [＿｜＿]     Date work carried out [＿｜＿]

Brief description

[＿＿＿＿＿＿＿＿＿＿＿＿]
[＿＿＿＿＿＿＿＿＿＿＿＿]
[＿＿＿＿＿＿＿＿＿＿＿＿]

**Tree surgeon**

## TREE SURGEON

*Company Name*

*Address*

Postcode

*Telephone No*                    Fax No

**Building regulations**

## BUILDING REGULATIONS

Building Control is a means to ensure that building work is carried out to approved standards and that safe and healthy conditions are provided for users of all buildings. Faulty work can affect the value of your property. The Building Regulations apply throughout the country. They cover structural stability, fire resistance, means of escape, drainage, ventilation, energy conservation and access for people with disabilities. Not all extensions or alterations require to be submitted for building regulations approval e.g: single storey additions not open to the house with a floor area less than 30 square metres such as conservatories, porches, covered yards or carports open on at least two sides; greenhouses solely for residential use; small detached buildings with a floor area of less than 15 square metres and containing no sleeping accommodation; detached buildings with a floor area less than 30 square metres containing no sleeping accommodation and either with brick or concrete walls or more than 1 metre from the boundary.

## Building regulations submission:

This is generally required for most alterations (not all). It is required for *all* structural alterations including openings between rooms, work involving drainage and other technical alterations. Where minor works are proposed and a competent, experienced builder is employed, a full submission may not be necessary and may be replaced with a Building Notice Submission. Note that Skip Permits must be obtained to place skips on the public highway. Information should be obtained from your local Building Control or Technical Services Department. Where approval has not been sought under Building Control and work has proceeded, a Regularisation Certificate may be sought retrospectively.

*Tick ☑ boxes, as appropriate*

Has an application been made for Building Regulations Approval?

Date of submission                    Satisfactory completion date

Application reference number

*See PLANNING AND BUILDING REGULATIONS APPROVALS in* **HOMEFILE**

**Repair and enforcement orders**

## REPAIR AND ENFORCEMENT ORDERS

Repair orders can be served under environmental health legislation and the Building Regulations. Stringent measures apply if repairs are not carried out where an order has been served and can mean a charge put on the property. However, grants may be obtained solely for repairs from the Environmental Health Department of your local council. (These are separate from House Renovation grants). Enforcement orders are served by the Housing Department where there is a breach of Planning Control.

Enter details, if applicable

## Dangerous structures:

Powers exist to remove dangerous buildings, walls and so forth, where people are at risk.

### NHBC WARRANTY

*Tick ☑ boxes, as appropriate*

Do you possess an NHBC 10-year warranty? ☐

Give description

| |
|---|
| |
| |
| |

*See NHBC WARRANTY CERTIFICATE in* **HOMEFILE** *... and see WARRANTY in* DIRECTORY

NHBC warranty

### LIFETIME HOMES

Is your home designed to accommodate changes in the future, such as: the addition of entrance level shower rooms and bedrooms, through-the-floor lift space? If so, enter details

| |
|---|
| |
| |
| |

Lifetime homes

### HOUSE RENOVATION GRANTS

If you have obtained a House Renovation Grant, state the purpose

| |
|---|
| |
| |

Date ☐☐☐     Reference number ☐

*See HOUSE RENOVATION GRANTS in* **HOMEFILE**

House renovation grants

## Types of grants:

There are four main types of grant for which you may apply, depending on whether you are an owner occupier, landlord, long-leaseholder or tenant. The grants system covers the following:

● Renovation Grants for repairs to remedy unfitness

● Common Parts Grants for one or more flats covering re-roofing, structural repairs and the improvements to communal halls and staircases in blocks of flats.

● Grants for Houses in Multiple Occupation.

● Disabled Facilities Grant for adaptations for a disabled occupant.

In addition to the above there is home repairs assistance. There is also an HEES Grant offered in conjunction with Renovation Grants and these are for loft insulation or energy efficiency measures including cavity wall insulation.

### What can be Included?

Repairs and improvements can cover replacement of missing amenities such as rotten windows and doors, ineffective damp-proof courses, unsatisfactory electrical wiring and defective rainwater pipes and gutters. They also cover repairs to defective roofs and timbers, walls and foundations, floors, staircases and wall and ceiling plaster. Kitchen, sanitary and drainage facilities can also be upgraded. Grants may cover home insulation and draught proofing, heating and improving the internal arrangement of the property.

### Professional Help

It is advisable to engage a professional, i.e: a qualified architect who is a member of the Royal Institute of British Architects, or a surveyor who is a member of the Royal Institution of Chartered Surveyors. It is also recommended that you select a builder who belongs to a trade association which operates a guarantee scheme such as those run by the Building Employers Federation and the Federation of Master Builders.

*See GRANTS in* DIRECTORY

## Advice:

Advice can be obtained from Advisory Centres and the Renovation Grants Section of your local council. You can also contact your Housing Advice Centre, Citizens Advice Bureau, Rent Office, Age Concern if you are elderly, the local library, banks and building societies. If you are disabled you can seek help from Social Services Departments or the Centre for Accessible Environments.

*See ADVICE in* DIRECTORY
*See CONSUMER HELP in* DIRECTORY

## Useful sources of information:

Various publications are available from the Department of the Environment or your local council. Professional advice is also available.

*See STATUTORY in* DIRECTORY
*See ARCHITECTS AND SURVEYORS in* DIRECTORY

# Section 6
# Construction

# Section Six | Construction

Double pitch with hip end    Double pitch with gable end    Single pitch    Valley    Mansard    Flat

**Figure 6.1**  Types of roof

## ROOF
*Tick ☑ boxes, as appropriate*

| | | | | |
|---|---|---|---|---|
| **Type** (Figure 6.1) | Double pitch ☐ | Single pitch ☐ | Valley ☐ | |
| | | Gable end ☐ | Hip end ☐ | |
| | Mansard ☐ | Flat ☐ | | |
| **Material** | Slate ☐ | Tile ☐ | Thatch ☐ | |
| | Felt ☐ | Bitumen ☐ | Composite ☐ | |
| | Lead sheet ☐ | Zinc sheet ☐ | | |
| **Features** | No. of ... Chimneys ☐ | Cowls ☐ | Vents/flues ☐ | |
| | Dormer windows ☐ | Skylights ☐ | Solar panels ☐ | |
| **Gutters** | Metal ☐ | Plastic ☐ | | |
| **Downpipes** | Metal ☐ | Plastic ☐ | | |

**Roof access**  If there is direct access for maintenance, state route

☐
☐

**Roof maintenance**  Provide details of works to roof, e.g. overhaul, reroofing, work to gutters etc

☐
☐

## EXTERNAL WALLS
*Tick ☑ boxes, as appropriate*

| | | | |
|---|---|---|---|
| **Construction** | Solid ☐ | Cavity ☐ | Timber framed ☐ |
| **Material** | Brick ☐ | Concrete block ☐ | Stone ☐ |
| | Slate ☐ | Concrete ☐ | Timber ☐ |
| | | Other ☐ | |
| **Wall finishes** | None ☐ | Smooth render ☐ | Timber cladding ☐ |
| | Stone cladding ☐ | Pebbledash ☐ | Cladding panels ☐ |

67

## Timber framed – vapour barrier:

Timber framed dwellings contain a vapour barrier normally consisting of polythene located behind the plasterboard. This is to prevent water vapour from inside the home reaching the timber frame. If you accidentally puncture it you should reseal it with masking tape, sealant or other suitable material.

**Entrance porch**

| **ENTRANCE PORCH** | | Tick ☑ boxes, as appropriate | |
|---|---|---|---|
| *Structure* | Open ☐ | Enclosed ☐ | |

**External doors**

| **EXTERNAL DOORS** | | | Tick ☑ boxes, as appropriate | | |
|---|---|---|---|---|---|
| *Type* | Double ☐ | Single ☐ | Sliding ☐ |
| | Stable ☐ | | |
| *Material* | Timber ☐ | UPVC ☐ | Metal ☐ |
| *Glazing* | Fully glazed ☐ | Half glazed ☐ | Non glazed ☐ |

**Windows**

| **WINDOWS** (Figure 6.2) | | | Tick ☑ boxes, as appropriate | | |
|---|---|---|---|---|---|
| *Opening* | Horizontal sliding ☐ | Side opening ☐ | Louvre ☐ |
| | Vertical sliding (sash) ☐ | Top opening ☐ | Pivot ☐ |
| | Fixed ☐ | | Trickle vent ☐ |

A trickle vent is a means of giving a small amount of ventilation by adjusting the setting of the window catch, or sliding a vent

| | | | Tick ☑ boxes, as appropriate | | |
|---|---|---|---|---|---|
| *Material* | Timber ☐ | UPVC ☐ | Metal ☐ |
| *Glazing* | Single ☐ | Double ☐ | Triple ☐ |
| | Secondary ☐ | Safety glass to low level ☐ | |

Homes which have single glazed windows generally result in condensation problems, excessive heat losses, wasted energy, poor comfort standards and avoidable carbon dioxide emissions to the atmosphere. Replacement with a reputable double glazing system not only reduces the above but can improve daylighting by allowing larger window areas, better use of the living space available and increased noise reduction. The European Union is likely to provide grants and programmes to encourage this environmental improvement.

**Internal walls**

| **INTERNAL WALLS** | | Tick ☑ boxes, as appropriate | |
|---|---|---|---|
| *Type* | Solid ☐ | Plasterboard ☐ | |

Type: A solid wall does not indicate whether the wall is loadbearing (i.e: supporting a floor or wall above it) or not. If you are contemplating making an alteration to this, consult an architect, structural engineer or reputable building contractor before you proceed.

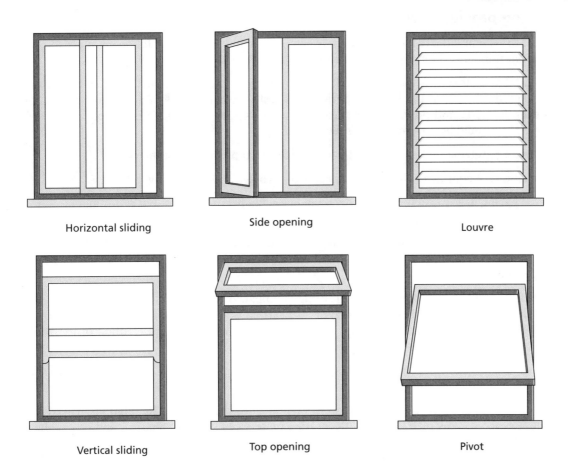

Horizontal sliding

Side opening

Louvre

Vertical sliding

Top opening

Pivot

**Figure 6.2** Types of opening windows

---

**INTERNAL DOORS**                                    *Tick ☑ boxes, as appropriate*

| | | |
|---|---|---|
| **Type** | Double ☐ Single ☐ | Sliding ☐ |
| | Bifolding ☐ | Room dividers ☐ |
| **Material** | Timber ☐ UPVC ☐ | Metal ☐ |
| **Glazing** | Fully glazed ☐ Half glazed ☐ | Non glazed ☐ |

**FLOORS**                                             *Tick ☑ boxes, as appropriate*

| | | |
|---|---|---|
| **Type** | Solid concrete ☐ | Suspended timber ☐ |
| **No. of storeys** | | Total number of storeys ☐ |
| | Basement ☐ Loft ☐ | Boarded loft ☐ |

*... See LIST OF BUILDERS, SUPPLIERS AND TRADE SPECIALISTS in* **HOMEFILE**

**Internal doors**

**Floors**

## Avoiding problems with builders:

In order to minimise the risk of disputes between owners and builders the following suggestions may be helpful. If in any doubt, consult a solicitor.

- Ensure that your contract with the builder fully describes the work to be carried out, the times of working, the length of the building period, any restrictions in terms of access and protection of existing property and provision for stage payments as each work stage is completed for a fixed price. This should be covered in the specification.

- Choose a reputable builder and ask for references from previous customers.

- Be cautious of contractors who offer to carry out work without charging VAT.

- Avoid paying in advance for more work than has actually been carried out or for materials not yet delivered.

- Ensure that a satisfactory final inspection has been carried out before the builder leaves the site. The completion certificate may then be obtained which is often required by solicitors when the property is sold.

- You, the owner, are responsible for ensuring compliance with the Building Regulations. It is in your interests to ensure that all inspections are carried out by the Building Control Surveyors as each appropriate work stage is completed because if a Notice of Contravention of the Building Regulations is issued it is served on the owner, not the builder.

- Failure to request inspections, especially a final inspection and drains test, is not only an offence, but can also affect any future sale of your property.

- Building Control Surveyors only control work subject to the Building Regulations. This does not include work such as plastering and decorating or services such as electrical and central heating work. This should be checked by yourself or by a professional adviser such as an architect or surveyor where they have been appointed by you.

- Ensure that insurance cover is adequate to cover the work being undertaken. Check the contractors public liability insurance is adequate and inform your own insurance company before any work begins.

- Ascertain that guarantees are adequate in terms of what they cover and the length of time.

- If work is not carried out to your complete satisfaction you should insist that defects are remedied. If this does not happen you should write to the contractor. If you are still not satisfied, you could employ another contractor and forward the charges to the original contractor but give them advance warning of your intention to do so.

## Homes of the future:

At present, the Government, the house construction industry, architects, researchers and the Peabody Trust are developing and building innovative homes of the future which will use technology to reduce costs, eliminate defects, minimise waste and save time. They will also be more tuned in to the consumers individual requirements and therefore will be more flexible. This could involve off site manufacturing, the use of components, re-useable materials and sustainable homes.

**Useful sources of information**

## USEFUL SOURCES OF INFORMATION

*See ARCHITECTS AND SURVEYORS in DIRECTORY*

*See BUILDERS in DIRECTORY*

*See CONSUMER HELP in DIRECTORY*

*See DOUBLE GLAZING in DIRECTORY*

*See ROOFING CONTRACTORS in DIRECTORY*

## External Finishes Schedule

Including roofs, gutters, downpipes, walls, windows, doors, paths and driveways.

### SUPPLIER

**Supplier**

| | |
|---|---|
| **Name** | |
| **Address** | |
| | |
| | Postcode |

| | | | |
|---|---|---|---|
| **Telephone No** | | Fax No | |
| **EMERGENCY No** | | e-mail address | |

### MANUFACTURER

**Manufacturer**

| | |
|---|---|
| **Name** | |
| **Address** | |
| | |
| | Postcode |

| | | | |
|---|---|---|---|
| **Telephone No** | | Fax No | |
| **EMERGENCY No** | | e-mail address | |

| Location | Item type | Style/Code No | Colour/Texture |
|---|---|---|---|
| | | | |
| | | | |
| | | | |
| | | | |
| | | | |
| | | | |
| | | | |
| | | | |
| | | | |
| | | | |

If receipts are available, where are they kept?

If samples or remnants are available, where are they kept?

## External Finishes Schedule

Including roofs, gutters, downpipes, walls, windows, doors, paths and driveways.

**Supplier**

### SUPPLIER

*Name*

*Address*

Postcode

*Telephone No*                    Fax No

*EMERGENCY No*                    e-mail address

**Manufacturer**

### MANUFACTURER

*Name*

*Address*

Postcode

*Telephone No*                    Fax No

*EMERGENCY No*                    e-mail address

| Location | Item type | Style/Code No | Colour/Texture |
|---|---|---|---|
|  |  |  |  |
|  |  |  |  |
|  |  |  |  |
|  |  |  |  |
|  |  |  |  |
|  |  |  |  |
|  |  |  |  |
|  |  |  |  |
|  |  |  |  |
|  |  |  |  |
|  |  |  |  |

If receipts are available, where are they kept?

If samples or remnants are available, where are they kept?

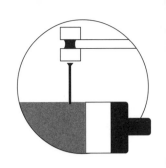

# Section 7
# Finishes, Fixtures and Fittings

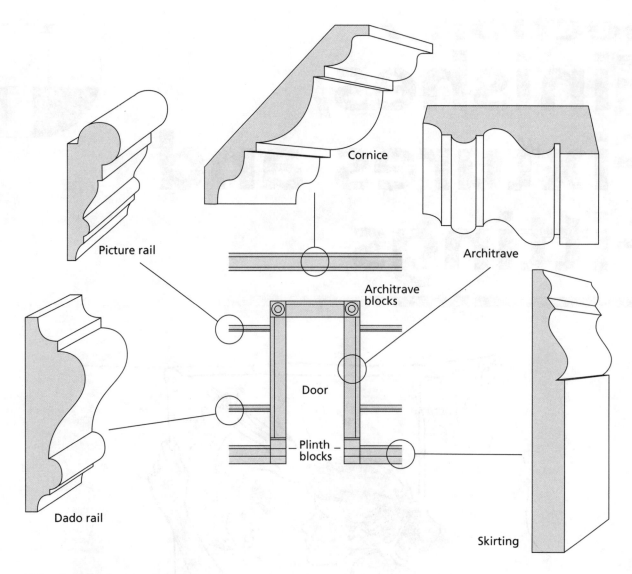

**Figure 7.1** Special features–details

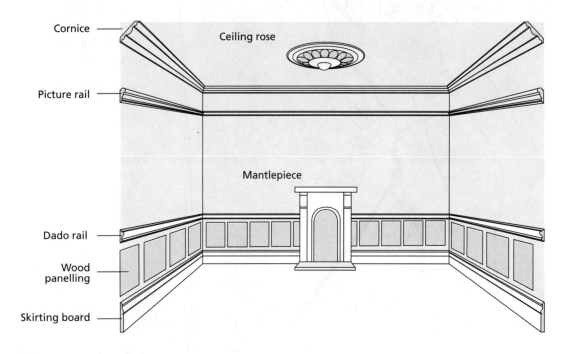

**Figure 7.2** Special features–room aspect

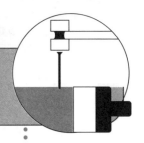

## Section Seven — Finishes, Fixtures and Fittings

### FINISHES AND SPECIAL FEATURES

*Tick ☑ boxes, as appropriate*

(Figures 7.1 and 7.2)

| | | | | |
|---|---|---|---|---|
| **Ceilings** | Ornamental and ceiling roses ☐ | | Suspended ☐ | |
| | Cornice/covings ☐ | | Illuminated ☐ | |
| **Walls** | Wall panelling ☐ | | Fabric wall covering ☐ | |
| **Decorative** | Moulding ☐ | Picture rails ☐ | Dado rails ☐ | |
| **Fire surround** | Marble ☐ | Cast iron ☐ | Timber ☐ | |
| | | | Stone ☐ | |
| **Windows and doors** | | Leaded ☐ | Stained glass ☐ | |
| | | | Serving hatch ☐ | |
| **Floors** | Ceramic tiles ☐ | Marble ☐ | Wood flooring ☐ | |
| | Parquet flooring ☐ | Linoleum ☐ | Sheet vinyl ☐ | |
| | | Vinyl tiles ☐ | Carpet ☐ | |

*See separate SCHEDULE A*

## Coding of valuables:

If you have any fixtures and fittings of special value, you may consider taking a photograph for insurance and security purposes. See Section **EIGHT – SECURITY REVIEW**.

### FIXTURES AND FITTINGS

*Tick ☑ boxes, as appropriate*

**Lighting** — *Please state the location of any of the following you may own*

| | |
|---|---|
| Recessed spot lights | |
| Surface spot lights | |
| Mirror lights | |
| Wall lights | |
| Fluorescent lights | |
| Dimmer switches | |
| Security lights | |

**Extractor fans**

| | | | | | |
|---|---|---|---|---|---|
| Kitchen ☐ | Utility room ☐ | Bathroom ☐ |
| Shower room ☐ | W.C. ☐ | |

| Other | Loft ladder ☐ | No of mirrors ☐ | No of Bathroom Cabinets ☐ |
|---|---|---|---|
| | No of venetian blinds ☐ | No of roller blinds ☐ | Heated airing cupboard ☐ |
| | Airing cupboard without heating ☐ | No of Fitted wardrobes ☐ | Recessed wall bed ☐ |

*See separate SCHEDULE B*

## Special needs facilities

### SPECIAL NEEDS FACILITIES

*Tick ☑ boxes, as appropriate*

| Ramps ☐ | Chairlift ☐ | Guardrails ☐ |
|---|---|---|
| Grabrails in bathroom ☐ | Tilting seat in bathroom ☐ | Disabled bath ☐ |

## Kitchen and utility fittings

### KITCHEN AND UTILITY FITTINGS

| Built-in oven ☐ | Built-in extractor hood ☐ | Built-in hobs ☐ |
|---|---|---|
| Built-in fixed base units ☐ | Built-in overhead units ☐ | Fitted tumble dryer ☐ |
| Single bowl sink ☐ | Double bowl sink ☐ | Waste disposal unit ☐ |
| Plumbed-in washing machine ☐ | | Plumbed-in dishwasher ☐ |

*See separate SCHEDULE C*

## Sanitary fittings and accessories

### SANITARY FITTINGS AND ACCESSORIES

*Tick ☑ boxes, as appropriate*

| Bath ☐ | Shower fitting ☐ | Separate shower enclosure ☐ |
|---|---|---|
| Power shower ☐ | Shower screen ☐ | Shower curtain ☐ |
| Bidet ☐ | Vanitory unit ☐ | Heated towel rail ☐ |

*See separate SCHEDULE D*

*See also INVENTORY OF COSTS.*

*See FITTINGS AND EQUIPMENT GUARANTEES, RECEIPTS, USER AND OPERATING INSTRUCTIONS in* **HOMEFILE.**

*See SAMPLES in* **HOMEFILE.**

*USEFUL SOURCES OF INFORMATION*

*See ARCHITECTS AND SURVEYORS in DIRECTORY.*

*See CONSUMER HELP in DIRECTORY.*

*See DECORATORS in DIRECTORY.*

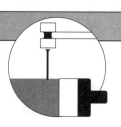

## Notes to Schedules

In addition to dealing with special features, you can use this section to keep a note of all of your household fixtures and fittings. For example, in relation to wallpaper or special wall coverings, you can note where you made your purchase, the name of the manufacturer, the style number, the colour/pattern and maybe even where you keep samples or remnants! In addition, by keeping your receipts and totalling your costs, you will ensure that your home is adequately insured.

For item type use the following abbreviations. Use the first letter, except in the case of windows and ceilings.

| | | |
|---|---|---|
| C = Carpet, | F = Flooring, | W = Wallpaper, |
| T = Tiling, | P = Painting, | Win = Windows, |
| D = Doors, | Ce = Ceilings | |

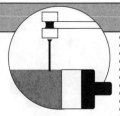

## Schedule A
## Finishes and Special Features

Including Carpets, Flooring, Wallpapers, Tiling, Painting, Windows, Doors and Ceilings.

**Supplier**

### SUPPLIER

*Name*

*Address*

Postcode

*Telephone No*            Fax No

*EMERGENCY No*            e-mail address

**Manufacturer**

### MANUFACTURER

*Name*

*Address*

Postcode

*Telephone No*            Fax No

*EMERGENCY No*            e-mail address

| Location/Room | Item Type | Style/Code No | Colour/Pattern | Quantity |
|---------------|-----------|---------------|----------------|----------|
|  |  |  |  |  |
|  |  |  |  |  |
|  |  |  |  |  |
|  |  |  |  |  |
|  |  |  |  |  |
|  |  |  |  |  |
|  |  |  |  |  |
|  |  |  |  |  |
|  |  |  |  |  |
|  |  |  |  |  |
|  |  |  |  |  |

If receipts are available, where are they kept?

If samples or remnants are available, where are they kept?

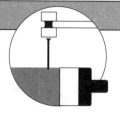

## Schedule A
## Finishes and Special Features

Including Carpets, Flooring, Wallpapers, Tiling, Painting, Windows, Doors and Ceilings.

### SUPPLIER

*Name*

*Address*

Postcode

*Telephone No*          Fax No

*EMERGENCY No*          e-mail address

Supplier

### MANUFACTURER

*Name*

*Address*

Postcode

*Telephone No*          Fax No

*EMERGENCY No*          e-mail address

Manufacturer

| Location/Room | Item Type | Style/Code No | Colour/Pattern | Quantity |
|---|---|---|---|---|
| | | | | |
| | | | | |
| | | | | |
| | | | | |
| | | | | |
| | | | | |
| | | | | |
| | | | | |
| | | | | |
| | | | | |

If receipts are available, where are they kept?

If samples or remnants are available, where are they kept?

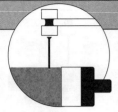

## Schedule A
## Finishes and Special Features

Including Carpets, Flooring, Wallpapers, Tiling, Painting, Windows, Doors and Ceilings.

**Supplier**

### SUPPLIER

| Name | |
|---|---|
| Address | |

Postcode

Telephone No     Fax No

EMERGENCY No     e-mail address

**Manufacturer**

### MANUFACTURER

| Name | |
|---|---|
| Address | |

Postcode

Telephone No     Fax No

EMERGENCY No     e-mail address

| Location/Room | Item Type | Style/Code No | Colour/Pattern | Quantity |
|---|---|---|---|---|
| | | | | |
| | | | | |
| | | | | |
| | | | | |
| | | | | |
| | | | | |
| | | | | |
| | | | | |
| | | | | |
| | | | | |
| | | | | |

If receipts are available, where are they kept?

If samples or remnants are available, where are they kept?

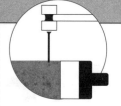

## Schedule B
## Fittings

Including Special Needs but not Kitchen or Sanitary.

### SUPPLIER

Supplier

Name

Address

Postcode

Telephone No

Fax No

EMERGENCY No

e-mail address

### MANUFACTURER

Manufacturer

Name

Address

Postcode

Telephone No

Fax No

EMERGENCY No

e-mail address

Location/Room

Type of fitting

Style/Code No              Colour/Finish

Guarantee Details                Expiry date

Location/Room

Type of fitting

Style/Code No              Colour/Finish

Guarantee Details                Expiry date

Location/Room

Type of fitting

Style/Code No              Colour/Finish

Guarantee Details                Expiry date

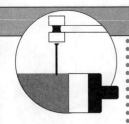

## Schedule B
## Fittings

Including Special Needs but not Kitchen or Sanitary.

**Supplier**

### SUPPLIER

*Name*

*Address*

Postcode

*Telephone No*          Fax No

*EMERGENCY No*          e-mail address

**Manufacturer**

### MANUFACTURER

*Name*

*Address*

Postcode

*Telephone No*          Fax No

*EMERGENCY No*          e-mail address

Location/Room

Type of fitting

Style/Code No          Colour/Finish

Guarantee Details          Expiry date

Location/Room

Type of fitting

Style/Code No          Colour/Finish

Guarantee Details          Expiry date

Location/Room

Type of fitting

Style/Code No          Colour/Finish

Guarantee Details          Expiry date

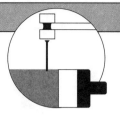

## Schedule C
## Kitchen and Utility Fittings

Supplier

### SUPPLIER

**Name**

**Address**

Postcode

**Telephone No**          Fax No

**EMERGENCY No**          e-mail address

Manufacturer

### MANUFACTURER

**Name**

**Address**

Postcode

**Telephone No**          Fax No

**EMERGENCY No**          e-mail address

Location/Room

Type of fitting

Style/Code No          Colour/Finish

Guarantee Details          Expiry date

Location/Room

Type of fitting

Style/Code No          Colour/Finish

Guarantee Details          Expiry date

Location/Room

Type of fitting

Style/Code No          Colour/Finish

Guarantee Details          Expiry date

83

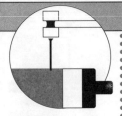

## Schedule C
## Kitchen and Utility Fittings

**Supplier**

### SUPPLIER

*Name*

*Address*

Postcode

*Telephone No*          Fax No

*EMERGENCY No*          e-mail address

**Manufacturer**

### MANUFACTURER

*Name*

*Address*

Postcode

*Telephone No*          Fax No

*EMERGENCY No*          e-mail address

Location/Room

Type of fitting

Style/Code No          Colour/Finish

Guarantee Details          Expiry date

Location/Room

Type of fitting

Style/Code No          Colour/Finish

Guarantee Details          Expiry date

Location/Room

Type of fitting

Style/Code No          Colour/Finish

Guarantee Details          Expiry date

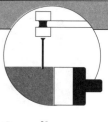

## Schedule D
## Sanitary Fittings

### SUPPLIER

Supplier

**Name**

**Address**

Postcode

**Telephone No**          Fax No

**EMERGENCY No**          e-mail address

### MANUFACTURER

Manufacturer

**Name**

**Address**

Postcode

**Telephone No**          Fax No

**EMERGENCY No**          e-mail address

Location/Room

Type of fitting

Style/Code No          Colour/Finish

Guarantee Details          Expiry date

Location/Room

Type of fitting

Style/Code No          Colour/Finish

Guarantee Details          Expiry date

Location/Room

Type of fitting

Style/Code No          Colour/Finish

Guarantee Details          Expiry date

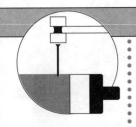

## Schedule D
## Sanitary Fittings

**Supplier**

### SUPPLIER

*Name*

*Address*

Postcode

*Telephone No*     Fax No

*EMERGENCY No*     e-mail address

**Manufacturer**

### MANUFACTURER

*Name*

*Address*

Postcode

*Telephone No*     Fax No

*EMERGENCY No*     e-mail address

Location/Room

Type of fitting

Style/Code No     Colour/Finish

Guarantee Details     Expiry date

Location/Room

Type of fitting

Style/Code No     Colour/Finish

Guarantee Details     Expiry date

Location/Room

Type of fitting

Style/Code No     Colour/Finish

Guarantee Details     Expiry date

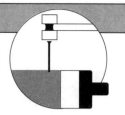

## Inventory of Costs

Use this sheet to list the major costs incurred in your household. A few items are already listed in the table. The figures to be entered in the cost boxes should be the total spent on that item. For other items use the blank boxes provided.

| Item/Fixture/Fitting | Cost |
|---|---|
| Carpets | |
| Flooring | |
| Wallpapering | |
| Tiling | |
| Painting | |
| Windows | |
| Doors | |
| Ceilings | |
| Electrical | |
| Kitchen/Utility | |
| Sanitary | |
| | |
| | |
| | |
| | |
| | |
| | |
| | |
| | |
| | |
| | |
| | |
| | |
| | |
| **Total** | |

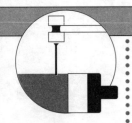

Notes

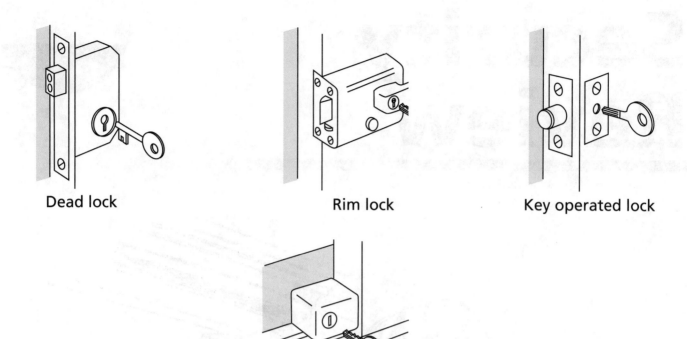

Dead lock

Rim lock

Key operated lock

Key operated patio door lock

**Figure 8.1**   Door locks

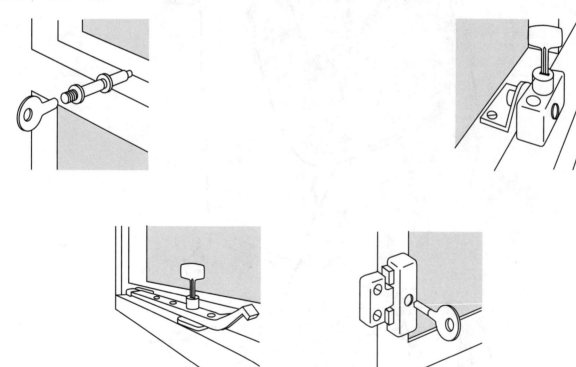

Key operated window locks

**Figure 8.2**   Window locks

---

### Passive Security Devices

## PHYSICAL MEASURES/LOCKS

If UPVC doors have been installed it is vital to ensure that any further security devices which you may feel are necessary do not invalidate your door guarantee. Contact the door manufacturer or consult the guarantee for advice on security matters. In addition, glass panels on doors, or adjacent to doors, should be laminated to prevent breakage. All locks should conform to BS3621/1980 and carry the BS kitemark.

### Main Entrance Door/Final Exit Door and Locks

These should be 44mm thick with rebated frames secured at 600mm centres in accordance with BS 8220. A five lever mortice deadlock or a Rim Automatic Deadlock complying with BS 3621 should be fitted. They should have two locking devices fitted one third from the top and one third from the bottom of the door – both operated by a key externally, and internally by a thumb turn, knob or lever handle – or a multi point locking system with a minimum of three locking points. The door should have three hinges and a door chain or limiter. Glazing should be laminated 6.4mm (quarter of an inch) thick.

*Tick ☑ boxes, as appropriate*

**Door material**      UPVC ☐      Timber ☐      Steel door and frame ☐

Glass panels in door or adjacent ☐

**Security**      5 lever mortice dead lock ☐

Hinge bolts ☐      Spy hole ☐      Door chain ☐

Secondary locks ☐      Steel reinforcing plate to lock edge of door ☐

Vision barrier to letterbox ☐      Secondary front door with additional lock ☐

*Door chains should be used when checking the identity of the caller at the door. They are not a permanent security measure to be used in place of locks. Additionally, letterboxes must comply with the Royal Mail British Standard.*

### Rear or Side Doors

Door thickness, frame, hinges and glazing should be as for front door. The door should have a single key operated dead lock and two key operated mortice bolts or two key operated dead bolts fitted one third from the top and one third from the bottom of the door – or a multi point locking system with three or more locking points.

Do all external doors have an adequate level of security, as above? ☐

### Sliding Patio Doors

These should have a multi point locking system with a minimum of three locking points using mushroom headed, hook or shoot bolts and an anti-lift device. Glazing requirements should be as for front doors.

Do patio doors comply with the above? ☐

**For the above refer to Figure 8.1**

## Garden and Boundary Gates

Garden and boundary gates should be as high as adjacent fencing and not be easy to climb. Interconnecting doors to garages should have fixings and locks as for front/rear doors.

If these doors exist, do they comply with the above? ☐

## Lower Floor Windows

For all opening windows on the ground floor, locks require a key operated deadlock, with a snap to lock and press to unlock action. Louvre windows must have their glass panels secured with adhesive to stop their removal from the frames.

Do all windows comply with these guidelines, or is there alternative satisfactory security?

Please give details and date of any remedial action [                    ]

[                    ]

Are there sliding grilles or shutters as extra security provisions? ☐

## Upper Floor Windows

For all upper floor windows, security measures must take into account fire brigade access, and use as an escape route in the event of fire.

Do all windows comply with these guidelines, or is there alternative satisfactory security?

Please give details and date of any remedial action [                    ]

[                    ]

**For the above refer to Figure 8.2**

## Boundary Security

Rear gardens should be secured with a robust fence or wall to a minimum height of 1.8 metres and a maximum of 2 metres, unless local planning regulations specify otherwise. Those backing on to footpaths or open spaces should be protected by an additional deterrent such as trellis. Any fence or wall where there is barbed wire must have a sign warning against possible injury. If this measure is not taken, legal action could be taken against you, the occupier. In addition, boundary walls, refuse enclosures, fuel bunkers, flat roofs and balconies should not provide climbing areas for intruders or give access to upper floors.

**Boundaries**

**BOUNDARIES**                                    *Tick ☑ boxes, as appropriate*

Fencing and trellis ☐                    Brick wall and trellis ☐

Anti-climb paint on top of walls ☐       If others exist, please enter details below

[                    ]

**Planting**

**PLANTING**

This must avoid the creation of potential hiding places for intruders. Frontages should be in open view and should not exceed 1 metre in height, that is, to avoid obscuring doors and windows. Attention should be given to the location gands species of trees, in order that they will not grow to obscure street lamps or become climbing aids. They should remain low and preferably have a thorn content.

Do you have deterrent bushes? ☐

## Design Matters

There should be no recessed doorways, or areas shielded from view which could hide intruders. However, since in some cases these are features of the property, occupiers should take precautions such as extra lighting to avoid concealed area dangers.

> If you need to take steps to avoid your entrance concealing intruders, enter details below, e.g. sufficient lighting.

## MANAGEMENT ITEMS

### Multiple-occupancy dwellings:

Common entrance door:
The door should be self-closing with a single, automatically deadlocked latch bolt, operated externally by a key and internally by a thumb turn, knob or lever handle. Also it should have electro-magnetic access control and an entry phone system. No more than eight flats should share a common entrance. If you live in a block of eight or more dwellings, the police recommend closed circuit television (CCTV) camera access.

Individual flat doors:
The door should have a single dead bolt, operated externally by a key and internally by a thumb turn, knob or lever handle, or a multi point locking system with a minimum of three locking points. It should also have three hinges and a door chain or limiter.

*Tick* ☑ *boxes, as appropriate*

In light of this, if security is to be reviewed, state plan of action.

For common areas, is there a 24 hour caretaker/security porter? ☐

Is there a separate key-operated letterbox for each dwelling? ☐

## LOCKSMITH COMPANY

*Name*

*Address*

Postcode

*Telephone No*          Fax No

*EMERGENCY No*          e-mail address

**Management items**

**Locksmith company**

| Active Security Devices |
| --- |

### ELECTRONIC

*Tick ☑ boxes, as appropriate*

**Electronic**

Electronic door entry system for individual houses or common shared entrances:

Visual ☐      Push-button ☐

Security cameras/CCTV ☐      Electronic boundary gates ☐

**Lighting**

### LIGHTING

*Tick ☑ boxes, as appropriate*

External security lights   Infra-red activated ☐   Time switch ☐   Photo-electric cell ☐

Internal security lights (for use during holidays or when absent from the home)

Delayed action/timer control plugged into socket ☐

Delayed action/timer wired into electrical installation ☐

**Alarm systems**

### ALARM SYSTEMS

These fall into two groups, wireless and wired systems. Wireless alarms conforming to BS 6799 use passive infra-red sensors and magnetic door and window contacts to detect movements. Such movements trigger signals which are sent by radio waves to a central control panel that activates the alarm. They are easy to install and can be taken with you if you move. Wired alarm systems have similar features but signals are transmitted by wires. Your alarm should be installed and maintained by an installer who is recognised by the National Advisory Council of Security Systems (NACOSS) or by an installer who is regulated by either the Security Systems and Alarm Inspection Board (SSAIB) or the Alarm Inspectorate and Security Council (AISC).

*Tick ☑ boxes, as appropriate*

Box without alarm bell ☐    Alarm contacts ☐    Pressure pads ☐

Box with alarm bell ☐    Panic button ☐    Infra-red ☐

Is the alarm centrally controlled ☐    Is the alarm of an audible type? ☐

Is your alarm NACOSS or SSAIB or AISC maintained? ☐

Do you know who to contact, how to activate and switch off your system? ☐

**Security system supplier**

### SECURITY SYSTEM SUPPLIER

| | |
| --- | --- |
| *Name* | |
| *Address* | |
| | |
| | Postcode |
| *Telephone No* | Fax No |
| *EMERGENCY No* | e-mail address |

## ALARM SYSTEM MAINTENANCE COMPANY

*Name*

*Address*

Postcode

*Telephone No*                    Fax No

*EMERGENCY No*                    e-mail address

*See SECURITY SYSTEMS USER INFORMATION in* **HOMEFILE.**

Alarm system maintenance company

Your local Police Station and Environmental Health Department *must* be informed of who your nominated keyholders are. If you wish to register this information below you may do so or alternatively, for security purposes, you may only wish to supply limited information.

## SECURITY ALARM KEYHOLDER NO 1    (a person other than the owner occupier)

*Name*

*Address*

Postcode

*Telephone No*

*Evening Telephone No*

Security alarm keyholder no 1

## SECURITY ALARM KEYHOLDER NO 2    (a person other than the owner occupier)

*Name*

*Address*

Postcode

*Telephone No*

*Evening Telephone No*

Security alarm keyholder no 2

The householder *must* ensure that the keyholder has full instructions on procedure if called out by the police when the alarm is activated; for instance how should the keyholder re-set the alarm.

**Neighbour-hood watch**

## NEIGHBOURHOOD WATCH

*Tick ☑ boxes, as appropriate*

Are you a member? ☐

If not, have you considered joining an existing group? ☐

Has your home been inspected by a Crime Prevention officer? ☐

Have you entrusted your keys and given full instructions to a key holder? ☐

Name _____ Telephone No ☐

Have you entrusted your keys to a bank, or safe deposit box? ☐

Your police station Crime Prevention Officer can provide you with leaflets giving details of fuller security.

**Coding of valuables**

## CODING OF VALUABLES

There are various ways of marking your valuables. Televisions, video recorders, computers and cameras can be engraved using a stencil and scribing tool which is indelible. Antiques and jewellery can have invisible marks using ultra-violet marking pens where the marks show only under ultra-violet lamps used by the police. However these marks need to be renewed from time to time. The Metropolitan Police now suggest that all items valued by their owner are photographed and marked with either an ultra-violet pen or 'smart water' or other such product. Smart water does not need to be renewed. All police stations in the Metropolitan area are now equipped with ultra-violet searching facilities for all property. The Association of British Insurers recommend photographing your valuables and recording the model and serial number of electrical goods. Some of the larger insurance companies are now offering a reduction in premium for any persons who can prove that they have photographed items of property that they are insuring.

The Metropolitan Police are now providing another service for all victims of crime. When 'identified' pieces of property are recovered by the police, they are now digitally imaged onto a computer database which can be searched by all victims of crime. The system is called the 'Bumblebee Property Bank' and it is currently situated at New Scotland Yard. An appointment can be made to view the images on the database. Very soon the same facility will be available throughout the Greater London Metropolitan Police area.

*Tick ☑ boxes, as appropriate*

Have you marked your valuables for identification, e.g. with a postcode or date of birth? ☐

Do you display a window sticker to advise that your possessions are marked? ☐

Where items such as jewellery, antiques etc are not marked, have you recorded hallmarks, identifying marks or scratches? ☐

Are the items photographed? ☐

Are serial numbers, make and model recorded and stored in a safe place? ☐

*The photographing of valuables can assist the Police in the recovery of stolen items via their computer system. See SECURITY in DIRECTORY*

# Section 9
# Health and Safety

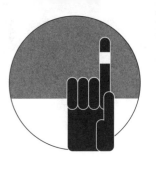

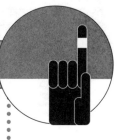

### Fire Precautions

Fires are caused deliberately or accidentally. Some of the causes include human error, faulty electrical installations and faulty gas supplies, cooking appliances, unguarded fireplaces or careless smokers. Hazards can be reduced by unplugging electrical appliances after use and sweeping chimneys regularly. The speed at which a fire spreads can also be affected by the presence of highly flammable materials in the home and the storage of hazardous substances, e.g: paint, fuels and chemicals. These should be confined to outbuildings.

## PHYSICAL PROTECTION

**Physical protection**

To help you in the event of fire, protective measures are detailed. In the case of buildings divided into flats or houses where lofts are converted i.e. above three storeys, fire doors may be required to certain parts of the dwelling (consult the local Building Control officer). Doors have different fire ratings as appropriate. A fire door comprises an appropriate sized timber door frame, an appropriate seal that expands on reaction with heat (i.e. intumescent) and where appropriate, sufficiently sized and constructed glazed openings or vision panels within doors. Fire separation materials will be required between two adjacent flats in the floors and/or walls. Also, fire separation may be required within flats to high risk areas such as kitchens, living rooms, bedrooms and to protect escape routes i.e. halls and staircases.

There are more specific requirements for fire precautions and for safety in certain existing homes in multiple occupation, hostels and for tower blocks of flats. These include the provision of fire-fighting stairs and lifts, dry risers to assist fire-fighting and external escape stairs. Special provisions are necessary for residential care premises, including the use of chair lifts and for evacuating disabled people.

---

*Tick ☑ boxes, as appropriate*

| | | |
|---|---|---|
| **Door and frames** | Fire rated door frames ☐ | Self closing fire rated doors ☐ |
| | | Fire seals to door frames ☐ |
| **Glazing** | | Georgian wired glass vision panels to fire doors ☐ |
| **Fire linings** | Fire lining to staircase ☐ | Fire lining between adjacent rooms ☐ |
| **Equipment** | Fire extinguisher ☐ | Fire blanket ☐ |

*Fire blankets to be to BS 6575 and should be kept in the kitchen.*

---

*See FIRE PRECAUTIONS USER INFORMATION in* **HOMEFILE**

## FURNITURE AND FURNISHINGS

**Furniture and furnishings**

From December 1996 anyone letting property, houses, flats and holiday homes containing furniture which does not display a label indicating that it is fire retardant (i.e. in accordance with the 1988 Fire Safety Regulations), can be prosecuted. This applies to upholstery including chairs, sofas, mattresses and headboards. The liability extends to the owner, landlord and managing agent. It will also apply to items on sale. Generally the furniture affected contains foam and applies from the 1950s onwards.

Does your home contain fire retardant upholstery? ☐

**Fire extinguishers**

## FIRE EXTINGUISHERS

Fire extinguishers should conform to BS EN3 or BS 7863 and have a kitemark or the special BAFE mark.

If your home has a fire extinguisher it should only be used to tackle a fire in its very early stages. You should always put your own and other people's safety first. Make sure you can escape if you need to, never block a fire exit and never let the fire develop to such a stage as could block your exit. If you cannot put out the fire or the extinguisher becomes empty, get out and get everyone out of the building. Close all doors behind you as you go. Then telephone the fire brigade.

Note: *Changes to colour coding for fire extinguishers*
From January 1997 the body colour of all new fire extinguishers supplied in the EC became signal red. In the UK a colour zone of up to a MAXIMUM 5% of the surface area of the extinguisher body may be used to identify the extinguishing agent.

Fuller information is available from the leaflet 'Fire safety in the Home – How to choose and use fire extinguishers for the home'. Contact the communication directorate at the Home Office or your local fire brigade for details.

In addition an extinguisher should be in a place where it can be reached quickly. The best place is on an escape route, that is, near an outside door, from the living areas to an outside door, or adjacent to a specific risk. It should be properly fixed to the wall at a height where it can be reached. It should be kept out of the reach of children.

Fire extinguishers should be fixed where they can be easily seen. Putting them inside cupboards or behind doors will only waste time if fire breaks out. They should not be placed over cookers or heaters or in places of extreme temperatures.

| | | | *Tick ☑ boxes, as appropriate* | |
|---|---|---|---|---|
| **Type** | Water (red) | ☐ | Multi-purpose dry powder (blue) | ☐ |
| | AFFF (cream) | ☐ | Standard dry powder (blue) | ☐ |
| | Foam (cream) | ☐ | $CO_2$ (black) | ☐ |
| **Location** | Location of fire extinguisher | | | |

In the event of using a fire extinguisher, always call the Fire Brigade, even though the fire has been put out. As experts, they will ensure that the fire is properly extinguished.

## Maintenance

Fire extinguishers should be serviced once a year by a company registered with the British Approvals for Fire Equipment (BAFE). They must also be recharged, whether they are only partially used, or are full.

**Fire equipment servicer**

Date of servicing extinguisher ☐

### FIRE EQUIPMENT SERVICER

| | |
|---|---|
| **Name** | |
| **Address** | |
| | |
| | Postcode |
| **Telephone No** | Fax No |
| **EMERGENCY No** | e-mail address |

*See FIRE EXTINGUISHERS in* **HOMEFILE**

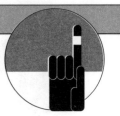

## SMOKE ALARMS

### Electronic

You should always buy an alarm which meets BS 5446 Part 1. It should be fitted on the ceiling near to the centre of the room at least 30 cms (12 inches) away from any wall or light fitting. If your home is a multi floor dwelling, one alarm should be fitted at the bottom of the staircase with an alarm on each upstairs landing. If only one alarm is fitted it should be in a place where it can be heard throughout the home, particularly when you are asleep. An alarm should not be fitted in the kitchen or bathroom.

You should check the battery once a month by pressing the test button. Also once a year you should change the battery and vacuum the inside of the alarm to prevent dust blocking the sensor chamber.

The Royal National Institute for the Blind can clarify any special requirements for the blind.

**Smoke alarms**

*Tick ☑ boxes, as appropriate*

| | | |
|---|---|---|
| *Type* | Battery operated ☐ | Mains operated ☐ |
| *Location* | Location of smoke alarm | ☐ |
| *Operation* | How to activate/switch off | ☐ |
| *Maintenance* | Does your smoke alarm and maintenance routine comply with the guidelines? | ☐ |
| | Date of change of battery | ☐ |

*See SMOKE ALARMS in* **HOMEFILE**

*See SPECIAL NEEDS in* **DIRECTORY**

## FIRE ALARMS

**Fire alarms**

Profoundly deaf people may need specific types of alarm signal e.g. lights or other visual signs, vibrating devices or sound signals within carefully selected frequency bands. Technical advice on the selection of suitable devices can be obtained from the Royal National Institute for the Deaf

*Tick ☑ boxes, as appropriate*

Fire alarm box ☐

| | | |
|---|---|---|
| *Location* | Location of fire alarm | ☐ |
| *Operation* | How to activate/switch off | ☐ |
| *Maintenance* | Frequency of servicing | ☐ |

## FIRE ALARM SYSTEM SUPPLIER

**Fire alarm system supplier**

| | |
|---|---|
| *Name* | |
| *Address* | |
| | |
| | Postcode |
| *Telephone No* | Fax No |
| *EMERGENCY No* | e-mail address |

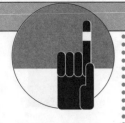

**Fire alarm service company**

## FIRE ALARM SERVICE COMPANY

| | |
|---|---|
| *Name* | |
| *Address* | |
| | |
| | Postcode |

| | | | |
|---|---|---|---|
| *Telephone No* | | Fax No | |
| *EMERGENCY No* | | e-mail address | |

*See FIRE ALARMS in* **HOMEFILE**

*See SPECIAL NEEDS in* **DIRECTORY**

**Fire and electrical safety**

## FIRE AND ELECTRICAL SAFETY

Some electrical appliances can be left on all the time while others should be switched off and unplugged when not in use. The manufacturer's instructions should be checked. Three-pin plugs should conform to the British Standard and carry the Kitemark and should not be removed by pulling the flex cable. Overloading a socket using several adaptors can cause it to overheat and catch fire and therefore a good quality adaptor with the correct fuse should be used. New equipment should have a BEAB mark of Safety, which means that it has been approved by the British Electrotechnical Approvals Board.

Signs which indicate *dangerous wiring* include: *hot plugs and sockets*, *fuses which blow* for no obvious reason, *lights flickering* and *brown scorch marks* on sockets and plugs.

For assistance contact your local electricity board; or an electrician on the roll of the National Inspection Council for Electrical Installation Contracting.

For further information and advice on fire safety in your home, contact your local fire brigade. In addition various pamphlets are available from the Home Office Fire Safety Unit.

*See FIRE SAFETY in* **DIRECTORY**

Does your home safety comply with the guidelines above? ☐

### Means of Escape

1. In case of fire breaking out in your home, you should plan your escape route *NOW* and familiarise yourself with fire procedures.

2. If you can do so, you should close the door of the room where the fire has broken out and close all other doors behind you. This will help delay the spread of fire and smoke.

3. Before opening a closed door use the back of your hand to touch it. Don't open it if it feels warm.

4. Get everyone out as quickly as possible. Don't try to pick up valuables or possessions. Make your way out as safely as possible and try not to panic.

5. Telephone the fire brigade on *999* from the nearest telephone and state address of fire clearly.

6. Never go back into your home until a fire officer has told you that it is safe.

Describe the clear escape route

Describe an alternative route

Give details of secondary stairs, or alternative means of escape, for homes above three storeys.

1. If cut off by fire, close door nearest to the fire and use towels or sheets to block any gaps. This will help stop smoke spreading into the room.
2. Go to the window. If the room is smoky, go down to the floor level where it is easier to breathe as smoke rises upwards.
3. Open the window and attract attention. Wait for the fire brigade.
4. If in immediate danger drop cushions or bedding to the ground to break your fall from the window.
5. Get out feet first and lower yourself to the full length of your arms before dropping.

Having read the above have you understood the guidelines?

## Structural Safety

**EVIDENCE OF PROBLEMS**                    *Tick ☑ boxes, as appropriate*

Signs of cracks/settlement ☐          Badly fitting doors/windows ☐

**POSSIBLE CAUSES**

Mining subsidence ☐                                Land heave ☐

Expansion and contraction of subsoil due to weather conditions ☐

Disturbance due to tree roots ☐          Buildings constructed on landfill sites ☐

Deficient support structures, e.g. beams/lintels ☐

*If problems are found, we recommend that a structural survey be undertaken.*

**Evidence of problems**

**Possible causes**

*See STRUCTURAL ENGINEERS in DIRECTORY*

*For guidance on categories of structural defects see STRUCTURAL SAFETY in DIRECTORY*

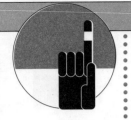

**Electricity**

**Noise**

## Environmental Aspects – External

### ELECTRICITY
*Tick ☑ boxes, as appropriate*

Adjoining overhead power line ☐     Adjoining electricity substation ☐

### NOISE

*From adjoining transport* Rail ☐     Road ☐     Air ☐

From other buildings ☐     Security alarms ☐

Does your intruder alarm have a cut out device to silence the alarm after a maximum period of 20 minutes? ☐

Have you notified your local Police Station and Environmental Health Department of two keyholders to attend your premises? ☐

*See also ALARM SYSTEMS in Section Eight SECURITY REVIEW*

### Noise pollution:

External noise can originate from aircraft, road traffic, loud car stereos, car alarms, motorbikes revving, loudspeakers used during 'unsocial hours' and even house alarms that go off while the owner is away and where they have not advised the police or the local council of at least two key-holders. If you have cause to complain you should first contact your local council environmental health department who can serve an abatement notice or you can complain directly to the Magistrates Court under section 82 of the Environmental Protection Act 1990 or you can take civil action. Controls can include local authority Bye-laws, Noise Abatement Zones, controls to reduce noise from building work, roadworks, demolition etc (the latter comes under the Control of Pollution Act 1974). Road traffic noise from exhausts or running engines is controlled by the Motor Vehicles Construction and Use Regulations 1986. The road traffic Act 1972 controls the type of car horn and when it can be used. Grants may be given to insulate homes beside busy roads and compensation may be given if your property depreciates in value.

There are restrictions on aircraft noise at Heathrow, Gatwick and Stansted airports including the routing of aircraft, maximum noise limits for departing aircraft and night flying. Noise insulation schemes may be available in order to give double glazing to your home. There are also bodies to whom you can complain in respect of helicopters, military aircraft and railways.

*See NOISE POLLUTION in DIRECTORY*

**External lighting**

### EXTERNAL LIGHTING
*Tick ☑ boxes, as appropriate*

Is your house affected by powerful lights? e.g. lighting masts to sports stadia ☐

Goods marshalling yards ☐     Adjacent buildings ☐

Security lighting ☐

### Light pollution:

Artificial light can safeguard and enhance our night time environment, but, if it is not properly controlled, it can be obtrusive and can cause serious physiological and ecological problems. 'Light Pollution' is caused by badly aligned sensor-activated domestic security lighting which affects neighbouring premises, excessively bright or badly positioned lights on commercial premises (usually on facades or car parking areas) and glare from sports field floodlighting.

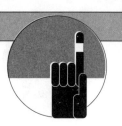

Three problems can arise from excessive numbers or excessive brightness of lights:

- Annoyance or disturbance due to 'glare' and 'light trespass'

- Energy wastage, i.e. due to consumption of electricity and emissions of green house gases and therefore a waste of money

- 'Sky glow' which masks the stars

There are not as yet any legal powers available to Environmental Health Officers to deal with such complaints as 'statutory nuisances' although lobbying may cause 'light pollution' to be added to the list of statutory nuisances contained in the Environmental Protection Act, 1990.

Much improvement can be achieved if lights are of an intensity that suits the task, if they are directed to cast light downwards, if they are shielded by the appropriate hood and if the sensor is adjusted so that they are not constantly being activated. The Institution of Lighting Engineers has produced guidance notes on this matter. If you experience 'light pollution' you can contact the Environmental Health Department of your local council. They may have a Light Pollution Unit who can intercede between neighbours.

*See LIGHT POLLUTION in* DIRECTORY

---

**PRIVACY**                                                   *Tick ☑ boxes, as appropriate*          **Privacy**

Is any part of your home affected by higher buildings? ☐

or by adjacent buildings? ☐

**FLOODING**                                                                                          **Flooding**

Coastal/tidal ☐          Flooding due to flood plain/low lying land ☐

Describe form of coastal or river flood protection ☐

☐

---

Information on flood deterrent schemes and also water purity and supply can be obtained from the Environment Agency which succeeded the former National Rivers Authority in April 1996.

*See FLOOD PROTECTION in* DIRECTORY

## TOXIC OR HAZARDOUS SUBSTANCES

**Toxic or hazardous substances**

### Asbestos:

Asbestos is a fibrous material which is found in three major forms: blue, brown and white. All of these forms are harmful to health if the asbestos fibres are breathed in and there is no cure. Asbestos has been used in a number of building materials and consumer products. It was used in insulation panels and in lagging for boilers, flues and pipes, roof and wall cladding as well as in products such as fire blankets, oven seals and ironing boards predominately in the 1950s and 1960s. Most uses of asbestos have now stopped and the remaining products which contain asbestos are labelled as such.

Asbestos materials only pose a risk to health when they are releasing fibres. Materials which are in good condition and are not releasing fibres should not be removed or disturbed. Damaged materials should be repaired or, if necessary, removed. However, removal can lead to the release of high levels of asbestos fibres and so should not be attempted before seeking expert advice. Contact your local council's Environmental Health Officer for advice on how to manage asbestos in your home. Samples should only be taken for testing by approved laboratories or analytical research chemists who are accredited by the UK Accreditation Service (UKAS). Disposal of asbestos waste is controlled by the Special Waste Regulations 1996. Asbestos must be removed by licensed contractors i.e. those licensed by the Asbestos Licensing Regulations Act 1983.

### Methane:

A certain amount of methane gas may be found in public sewers but should not affect the householder. It can also be found with other gases on landfill sites or where items have been buried for a

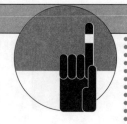

period of time and decomposition has occurred. Landfill gas only affects buildings close to landfill sites. Housing developments should comply with the requirements of the Building Regulations and these are now more stringent. Where a problem occurs detectors and vents can be fitted to protect the property. If in any doubt contact your local authority Building Control or Environmental Health Department.

## Radon gas:

Radiation is a fact of life and everyone is exposed to both natural and man-made sources of ionising and non-ionising radiation. In the UK, the National Radiological Protection Board (NRPB) keeps all sources of exposure under review and provides advice and free literature. Approximately 85% of all radiation received by the public is from natural sources, in the main from radon arising from within the home. In parts of the UK where NRPB has found homes to have high radon measurements, in particular in Cornwall, Devon and Northamptonshire, householders have been advised to undertake remedial action to reduce the risk of lung cancer. However, high radon measurements have been found in a considerable number of other areas in the country and householders can avail themselves of free information about radon by contacting the NRPB. In these instances, devices can be placed in the home to detect the gas and to pump it away.

Media and public concern has been raised over the last few years in the non-ionising field, which includes electromagnetic radiation (power lines and substations) and radiowaves (mobile phones and base stations). NRPB has responded to this concern by producing free literature on all these and other radiation topics.

---

**Do any of the following apply to your home?**          *Tick ☑ boxes, as appropriate*

Asbestos ☐          Methane gas ☐          Radon gas ☐

Gas/odours from landfill site ☐

Has asbestos been safely removed? ☐

---

## Smoke control:

Despite the improvements to air purity achieved by the Clean Air Acts of 1956 and 1968, about 22% of the smoke in our atmosphere comes from domestic sources. Dense domestic smoke can still obscure winter sunshine, contribute to fogs and cause respiratory problems for children, old people and those with bronchitis or asthma. The Clean Air Act 1993 has led to the creation of smoke control areas and smoke control programmes and has helped the UK meet European Union standards. Smoke control areas prohibit the emission of smoke from chimneys of dwellings and control smoke from industrial or commercial premises. The effect on domestic open fires can be that a more modern appliance should be installed that burns solid smokeless fuel. Your local authority may help with a grant of up to 70% of the total cost if you have to alter or replace an existing fireplace. There are penalties for householders who do not comply with the Clean Air Act.

## Garden bonfires:

These may be a convenient way of disposing of rubbish but they can cause a nuisance to neighbours and a hazard to passing traffic. They can release poisonous carbon monoxide and other irritating compounds. Some materials can explode or spread fire. Some materials are better composted, recycled or collected. Some bonfires can be classed as a nuisance under the Environmental Protection Act 1990.

## Air purity:

Indoor air purity can be affected by our activities, heating or ventilation appliances and from the structure or furnishings of the building. Modern building materials, furnishings and cleaning and decorating products also contaminate our environment. Solvents, paints, pesticides, deodorants etc can cause many health problems. Also suspect are some of the alternatives to asbestos, for example glassfibre and mineral wool. Formaldehyde used in wood products can affect health. The type of cavity wall insulation should be chosen with care. Active and passive smoking of cigarettes indoors puts health at risk.

Gas cookers, solid fuel fires, gas and paraffin heaters and wood stoves can be pollutants if not properly vented. Contaminants in the air such as mould, spores, viruses and bacteria can cause illness and allergic reactions.

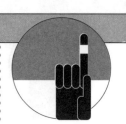

## Lead in Paints:

Lead is a hazardous substance and lead-based paint can be found in pre-1960 buildings. Removal by blasting, burning, scraping and power tool cleaning can contaminate the home and furnishings. Other sources are air pollution from leaded petrol, lead water pipes, food, hobbies and occupations involving lead. Lead residues can be accumulated over a lifetime and children and pregnant women should not be near renovation work involving the disturbance of lead based paint.

Its use was controlled from 1922 onwards through regulations and from the 1950s it was replaced by alternative white pigments in top coats and primers. Lead based paint may still be present beneath layers of lead free paint, particularly on internal doors and architraves and some exterior surfaces. Lead Test Kits are available from trade counters and merchants.

Lead waste should be disposed of in accordance with the Waste Management Licensing Regulations 1994 and the Environmental Protection (Duty of Care) Regulations 1992. A specialist should be used to remove lead, so as to minimise dust. They should use appropriate methods to either encapsulate the lead or to remove the item together with its lead paint intact (e.g. doors and windows) or to safely strip the lead from its background. There are stringent requirements to cover over all surfaces during removal and to clean up after removal has taken place.

Has lead paint been safely removed? ☐

## Household waste:

All waste is potentially dangerous whether through poisonous substances such as mercury and cadmium from batteries, old medicines, household cleaning and decorating chemicals and garden chemicals. Over 90% of domestic waste is disposed of in landfill sites which can cause local traffic noise, smells, wind borne litter, pests and flies, and decomposition can cause large amounts of carbon dioxide and methane. These are 'greenhouse' gases which contribute to global warming. Chemicals are also discharged into surrounding soil and cause contamination of ground water. However, in the future, landfill gas may be exploited as a source of energy. Less than 6% of domestic waste is incinerated, but emission of acid, chemicals and metals have to be controlled. Potentially they could generate electricity and heat.

Problems of waste disposal can be minimised by recycling and re-use, for example, glass, metal cans, textiles, plastics, paper and board and vegetable waste. By the year 2000, Government policy aims to recycle half of the potential recyclable household waste.

## Water pollution:

This can occur due to pollutant spillages or suspected pollution. Causes can include poorly maintained drains, gutters and downpipes, or because oil has been poured into the gutters, drains or road gullies, or because internal utilities such as toilets, washing machines, dishwashers and baths have been connected to surface water drains instead of foul water drains. If you suspect that your local river has become polluted contact your local council Environmental Health Department or your local Water Supply Company.

*See HAZARDOUS SUBSTANCES in* DIRECTORY

*See AIR PURITY in* DIRECTORY

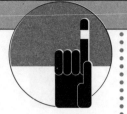

**Condensation/ mould**

## Environmental Aspects – Internal

### CONDENSATION/MOULD

This can be caused by sealed rooms due to double glazing and draught proofing, cold windows, sealing of chimneys/flues, lack of extraction and the generation of steam, etc in kitchens and bathrooms. Condensation will be reduced by extraction fans, opening windows, closing bathroom and kitchen doors, drying laundry outdoors wherever possible and avoiding the use of portable fuel heaters.

*Tick ☑ boxes, as appropriate*

EVIDENCE OF PROBLEMS ☐

REMEDIES  Natural ventilation, e.g. airbricks for underfloor ventilation ☐

Airbricks for room ventilation ☐  Fireplaces with unobstructed chimneys ☐

Mechanical ventilation – extractor fans ☐

**Damp**

### DAMP

Signs of this are a damp, musty smell, damage to, and discolouration of, decorations. This is termed rising damp, although the causes can be from defective damp proof courses, bridging of the damp course externally by soil or rubble and leaks in rainwater goods. Remedies include physical repair of damp proof courses, re-rendering external plinths and chemical damp proof course injection. A 9 inch (225mm) solid wall can take up to a year to thoroughly dry out residual moisture following damp proof course injection. In addition when damp proof replastering occurs internally normally to a height of one metre along the length of the injected wall, then redecoration with wallpaper should wait for at least six months. Walls can however, be decorated earlier than this, using emulsion paint.

*Tick ☑ boxes, as appropriate*

EVIDENCE OF PROBLEMS ☐

REMEDIES  Chemical damp proof course insertion ☐

Physical damp proof course insertion ☐  Damp proof plaster repairs to walls ☐

*See DAMP COURSE AND WOOD TREATMENT in DIRECTORY*

**Timber decay**

### TIMBER DECAY

Signs of decay include a musty smell, the presence of fungus and spores and the cracking, crumbling and rotting of timber thereby weakening its strength. The treatment by spraying timber is usually carried out by water based spray rather than solvent because of the danger of airborne spread of the solvent onto food surfaces, into socket outlets and in the air. The occupant still needs to be out of the premises when water based treatment is used and all carpets and floor coverings have to be taken up.

*Tick ☑ boxes, as appropriate*

EVIDENCE OF PROBLEMS  Woodworm ☐  Wet rot ☐  Dry rot ☐
infestation

REMEDIES  Chemical spray ☐  and/or replace affected timber ☐

*For details of survey reports, description of remedial works undertaken and certificates*

*See DAMP COURSE and WOOD TREATMENT DOCUMENTS in HOMEFILE*

*See DAMP COURSE AND WOOD TREATMENT in DIRECTORY*

## CARBON MONOXIDE POISONING FROM GAS FIRES  *Tick ☑ boxes, as appropriate*

Is your fire properly installed? ☐  Is your fire regularly serviced? ☐

Is the room adequately ventilated by means of floor or wall vents? ☐

## NOISE BETWEEN DWELLINGS  *Tick ☑ boxes, as appropriate*

EVIDENCE OF PROBLEMS ☐

Annoyance can be caused by loud and ill sited stereos, TV's, washing machines, hoovers, dogs left at home on their own, parties, DIY carried out at the crack of dawn or any activities that cause noise outside 'social hours'.

Is there airborne noise: audible voices, music etc? ☐

Is there impact noise: vibration from feet/furniture against walls/floors? ☐

SOLUTIONS:

*Sound insulation for airborne noise*

Dense material in walls ☐  Dense materials in floors (concrete) ☐

Double glazing ☐

Zoning of similar room functions together, e.g: halls, bedrooms, living rooms ☐

*Sound insulation for impact noise*

False or unconnected walls ☐  'Floating' or unconnected floors ☐

False ceilings ☐  Zoning of room functions as above ☐

*See NOISE POLLUTION in DIRECTORY*

## ENERGY EFFICIENCY  *Tick ☑ boxes, as appropriate*

EVIDENCE OF PROBLEMS ☐

Is the property too cold in winter and too hot in summer ☐

SOLUTIONS:

| | | |
|---|---|---|
| *Flat roofs* | Adequate thermal insulation | ☐ |
| *Pitched roofs* | Loft fitted with 100mm (4 inches) or more of insulation between joists | ☐ |
| *Walls* | Rigid board insulation | ☐ |

*Cavity walls*  Full cavity insulation ☐  Partial cavity insulation ☐

Injected foam insulation carried out by a BBA/BSI contractor ☐

Have you obtained an insulation certificate from your installer? ☐

*Ground floors*  Underfloor insulation laid between concrete slab and screed ☐

*Insulation of services*  Hot water cylinder ☐  Pipework ☐  Cold water tank ☐

*Adequate draught proofing*  Doors ☐  Windows ☐  Loft hatch ☐

*Draught lobbies to conserve heat*  Porch ☐  Conservatory ☐

*Energy rating*  Has your home been energy rated? ☐  Rating ☐

Carbon
monoxide
poisoning
from gas
fires

Noise
between
dwellings

Energy
efficiency

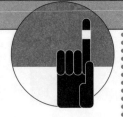

You may wish to contact the National Home Energy Foundation to obtain a national home energy rating (NHER). This assessment gives you the annual energy cost of your home.

Does your home possess an NHER report as stated above? ☐

## Energy efficiency, thermal insulation and draught proofing:

Where this is inadequate, grants may be possibly obtained either from your local council or from 'eaga' on behalf of the Home Energy Efficiency Scheme (HEES) which provides government grants. Various publications are available.

*See CAVITY WALL INSULATION CERTIFICATES and ENERGY RATING in **HOMEFILE***

*See ENERGY EFFICIENCY AND INSULATION in **DIRECTORY***

**Natural lighting**

## NATURAL LIGHTING

Windows within narrow/deep rooms appear to give less light than windows in wide/shallow rooms. Also, high window sills give less light but may give more privacy. Smaller windows, however, conserve more heat but may require excessive use of artificial lighting. Some tasks can be carried out using artificial light, others rely on good natural lighting.

### Child Safety

**Measures**

## MEASURES

The section deals primarily with young child safety. To protect your child from home hazards, safety equipment should have a British Standard label which means that the goods conform to a minimum level of quality and safety.

*Tick ☑ boxes, as appropriate*

| | |
|---|---|
| Fire doors to fireplaces ☐ | Fire guards ☐ |
| Cooker hob guard ☐ | Smoke detector in children's room ☐ |
| Childproof locks ☐ | Restraints on windows ☐ |
| Cupboard door latches ☐ | Dummy socket covers for electric points ☐ |
| Safety gates at the top and bottom of stairs ☐ | Adequate balcony rails ☐ |

Do you have a carbon monoxide detector to warn against defective fittings? ☐

Is there safety glass in or around doors, or safety film covering? ☐

## Cautionary Note:

Child Safety gates must be fitted in accordance with the manufacturers instructions and should be in accordance with the appropriate British Standard. It is recommended to carry out a regular check on the safety gate, to ensure all joints, screw fittings and the locking mechanism are secure and undamaged.

## Additional Note

### Health and Safety:

The Construction (Health, Safety and Welfare) Regulations 1996 (CHSW regulations) apply to all construction site work, including the construction of homes and set out physical standards and detailed ways of working in construction activities in order to achieve safety. They apply where new homes are being constructed and to alterations and extensions but not to DIY activities.

The Construction (Design and Management) Regulations 1996 (CDM regulations) deal with the planning of construction work, including homes if *five or more* people are involved in building the home, or the construction period involved is more than *30 days or 500 man-hours.*

Where existing property is being altered or extended, the application of the Health and Safety Regulations will depend on the nature of the work, on any items being disconnected, and the time spent carrying out the work.

When you are contemplating building work and are in any doubt regarding the application of the regulations, it is now your legal duty as the client/building owner to consult with your architect and/or the local office of the Health and Safety Executive, or the Technical Services Department of your Local Authority. Their telephone number and address can be found in the telephone directory.

*See HEALTH AND SAFETY in DIRECTORY*

*USEFUL SOURCES OF INFORMATION*

*See AIR PURITY in DIRECTORY*

*See STATUTORY in DIRECTORY*

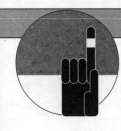

# Section 10
# Maintenance Diary

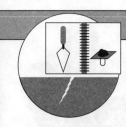

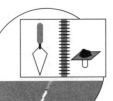

### Maintenance Diary

Use the Maintenance History and Reminder lists on the following pages to enter details of all regular activities and their corresponding costs. Alternatively you may wish to produce your own to be stored in your **HOMEFILE**. For costs relating to the home you may store relevant bills in your **HOMEFILE**. You may also wish to enter the names of contractors who carried out the work involved. You can also if you wish create extra pages of this in your **HOMEFILE**.

The following may help you in recognising the types of maintenance work that should be recorded in the Maintenance and History Reminder List.

## Activities could be grouped under the following headings:

### Statutory Payments
Council Tax, Water rates, TV licence, Car Tax etc.

### Insurance
Building, Contents, Life, Car, Health etc.

### Internal Maintenance of Household Items
Washing machine, boiler, carpet and upholstery cleaning, changing of batteries to smoke alarm, changing of filter to cooker extractor, cleaning of common areas in flats etc.

### External Building Maintenance
Roof, gullies, painting, drain clearance, external security gates, window cleaning and maintenance, chimney sweeping, swimming pool cleaning and maintenance, security alarms, maintenance of external parts of building and communal gardens in flats etc.

### Guidelines for Routine Maintenance

## Roofs

The surface of flat roofs should be protected before ladders are placed on them. Gutters should be cleaned annually. It is advisable to use a ladder with extension bracket to avoid damage to plastic gutters.

## Paintwork

Outside woodwork should be repainted or re-stained every four to five years to preserve the wood. This may need to be more frequent in marine atmospheres.

## Double Glazing

This should be carried out by a specialist using the appropriate glazing compounds and sealants.

## Manholes and Gullies

Manhole covers should be kept clear to assist maintenance. Gullies should be cleared at regular intervals.

## Damp-proof courses

You should ensure that soil and paving is 150mm (6 inches) below the damp-proof course and that air-bricks are kept unobstructed to assist ventilation beneath the floor.

## Trees

It is advisable to avoid planting trees close to your or your neighbours house, ancillary buildings or drains. This is especially so in clay soils where there are prescribed distances from buildings for planting certain species e.g. some are three quarters and some up to one and a quarter times the mature height from the building. Pruning and felling trees can also create swelling of soils and damage to foundations.

### Cautionary Note
Do not attempt any repair or maintenance work which may be too difficult for you or which involves a risk of falling from ladders. In these cases consult your builder.

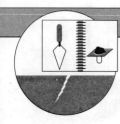

## Maintenance History and Reminder List

| Month/Year | Type of expenditure | Cost £ | Next Due |
|---|---|---|---|
| 05/95 | exterior painting | 1000 | 05/99 |
| | | | |
| | | | |
| | | | |
| | | | |
| | | | |
| | | | |
| | | | |
| | | | |
| | | | |
| | | | |
| | | | |
| | | | |
| | | | |
| | | | |
| | | | |
| | | | |
| | | | |
| | | | |
| | | | |
| | | | |
| | | | |
| | | | |
| | | | |
| | | | |
| | | | |
| | | | |
| | | | |
| | | | |
| | | | |
| | | | |
| | | | |
| | | | |
| | | | |
| Month/Year | Type of expenditure | Cost £ | Next Due |

## Maintenance History and Reminder List

| Month/Year | Type of expenditure | Cost £ | Next Due |
|---|---|---|---|
| 05/95 | exterior painting | 1000 | 05/99 |
|  |  |  |  |
|  |  |  |  |
|  |  |  |  |
|  |  |  |  |
|  |  |  |  |
|  |  |  |  |
|  |  |  |  |
|  |  |  |  |
|  |  |  |  |
|  |  |  |  |
|  |  |  |  |
|  |  |  |  |
|  |  |  |  |
|  |  |  |  |
|  |  |  |  |
|  |  |  |  |
|  |  |  |  |
|  |  |  |  |
|  |  |  |  |
|  |  |  |  |
|  |  |  |  |
|  |  |  |  |
|  |  |  |  |
|  |  |  |  |
|  |  |  |  |
|  |  |  |  |
|  |  |  |  |
|  |  |  |  |
|  |  |  |  |
|  |  |  |  |
|  |  |  |  |
|  |  |  |  |
|  |  |  |  |
|  |  |  |  |
|  |  |  |  |
|  |  |  |  |
|  |  |  |  |
|  |  |  |  |
| Month/Year | Type of expenditure | Cost £ | Next Due |

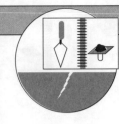

## Weekly Reminder List

To help you remember regular daily and weekly items and expenditures, here is a reminder list that could include paying for milk deliveries and newspapers, mobile library visits, delivery vans and others.

| | Activity | Cost |
|---|---|---|
| **Monday** | | |
| **Tuesday** | | |
| **Wednesday** | | |
| **Thursday** | | |
| **Friday** | | |
| **Saturday** | | |
| **Sunday** | | |

## Maintenance Contact List

**FUNCTION**

*Name*

*Address*

Postcode

*Telephone No*          Fax No

*EMERGENCY No*          e-mail address

**FUNCTION**

*Name*

*Address*

Postcode

*Telephone No*          Fax No

*EMERGENCY No*          e-mail address

**FUNCTION**

*Name*

*Address*

Postcode

*Telephone No*          Fax No

*EMERGENCY No*          e-mail address

**FUNCTION**

*Name*

*Address*

Postcode

*Telephone No*          Fax No

*EMERGENCY No*          e-mail address

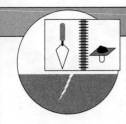

**FUNCTION**

*Name*

*Address*

Postcode

*Telephone No*                      Fax No

*EMERGENCY No*               e-mail address

---

**FUNCTION**

*Name*

*Address*

Postcode

*Telephone No*                      Fax No

*EMERGENCY No*               e-mail address

---

**FUNCTION**

*Name*

*Address*

Postcode

*Telephone No*                      Fax No

*EMERGENCY No*               e-mail address

---

**FUNCTION**

*Name*

*Address*

Postcode

*Telephone No*                      Fax No

*EMERGENCY No*               e-mail address

# The
# Directory

# The Directory

The following organisations either produce publications and give advice, or help you to contact professional or trade specialists. Other services include the Yellow Pages or the Blue Pages in your telephone directory, the Directory of Trade Associations in your local library, the nearest Citizens Advice Bureau or Housing Advice Centre

## ADVICE

Citizens Advice Bureaux
Refer to your local yellow pages for nearest office.

## AIR PURITY

**British Lung Foundation.**
78 Hatton Garden,
London, EC1N 8JR
Tel: 0171–831–5831

Regional Offices
South East – Tel: 0171–831–5831
Scotland – Tel: 0141–204–4110
Midlands – Tel: 0121–627–2260
North West – Tel: 0151–228–4723
South West – Tel: 0117–972–4858
North – Tel: 0191–263–0276

The above produces the booklet, 'Your home and your lungs – a guide to indoor air pollution'. It funds research into all lung conditions, provides public information and supports people affected by lung disease.

**The National Society for Clean Air and Environmental Protection (NSCA).**
136 North Street,
Brighton, BN1 1RG
Tel: 01273–326313

The above (see also under **NOISE POLLUTION**) produces the following booklets:

- 'Domestic Smoke Control'
- 'Indoor Air Pollution'
- 'Garden Bonfires'
- 'Household Waste'

## ARBITRATION

**The Chartered Institute of Arbitrators.**
International Arbitration Centre,
24 Angel Gate,
City Road,
London, EC1V 2RS
Tel: 0171–837–4483

The Chartered Institute of Arbitrators is an independent body which provides the means for consumers or commercial enterprises to settle their disputes through arbitration. The Institute is not an advisory body, and can only normally assist once the internal complaints procedure or conciliation procedure of the Trade Association has been exhausted. Initial contact should be made in writing, with a brief explanation of the type of dispute and what efforts have been made in order to settle the dispute.

## ARCHITECTS AND SURVEYORS

**Architects Registration Board (ARB).**
73 Hallam Street,
London, W1N 6EE
Tel: 0171–580–5861

The above maintains a list of members which may be used for verification purposes.

**Association of Consultant Architects (ACA).**
98 Hayes Road,
Bromley, BR2 9AB
Tel: 0181–325–1402
Fax: 0181–466–9079

The ACA publishes the following:

- 'The ACA Form of Building Agreement 1982 Third Edition 1998' and also a guide to this building contract.
- 'The ACA Form of Subcontract 1982 Third Edition 1998'
- 'ACA 98 – The Appointment of a Consultant Architect for small works'.
- 'Directory of Specialist Services provided by Architects'.
- 'Project Team Guidelines, Fee Negotiations and harmonised plans of work'.

**Royal Institute of British Architects (RIBA).**
66 Portland Place,
London, W1N 4AD
Tel: 0171–580–5533

- The Clients' Advisory Service can send you introductory leaflets on 'Working with your Architect'.
- The RIBA bookshop is open to the public and stocks the JCT Minor Works Contract.
- There is a mail order service from RIBA Publications, Finsbury Mission, Moreland Street, London, EC1V 8BB. (Tel: 0171–251–0791).
- The regional offices of the RIBA have lists of architects who deal with the smaller building projects.

**The Royal Incorporation of Architects in Scotland (RIAS).**
15 Rutland Square,
Edinburgh, EH1 2BE
Tel: 0131–229–7545

**Royal Society of Ulster Architects**
2 Mount Charles,
Belfast, BT7 1NZ
Tel: 01232–323760

**Royal Institution of Chartered Surveyors (RICS).**
Information Centre,
Surveyors Court,
Westwood Way,
Coventry, CV4 8JE
Tel: 01203–694757
Fax: 0171–334–3800

The above can offer advice over the telephone or help with the survey of a proposed property and it has a mail order service. There is also a bookshop at 12 Great George Street, London SW1P 3AD. Tel: 0171–222–7000 or 0131–225–7078. It also produces the detailed 'Guide to House Rebuilding Costs' published by the Building Cost Information Service.

## ARCHIVE

**Alan Godfrey Maps.**
12 The Off Quay Building,
Foundry Lane,
Newcastle, NE6 1LH
Tel: 0191–276 1155

The above provides maps for the majority, but not all, of the country.

## BUILDERS

**The Construction Confederation.**
Construction House,
56–64 Leonard Street,
London, EC2A 4JX
Tel: 0171–608–5000
Fax: 0171–608–5001

The above represents the interests of over 5000 construction companies and aims to help them improve their service to their clients. Among its members are the National Federation of Builders (tel: 0171–608–5150), and the House Builders Federation (tel: 0171–608–5100).

It has a guarantee scheme which is handled by the Building Guarantee Scheme UK Ltd. See address under **INSURANCE.**

**National Federation of Builders.**
56–64 Leonard Street,
London, EC2A 4JX
Tel: 0171–608–5150

The above provides the following:

- A list of builders in your area who can carry out the work that you require.

- A guide called 'Get The Best From Your Builder'

Members operate to a stringent code of conduct. Heightened vetting procedures have been brought in. A simplified building contract has been produced. Ten year guarantees are available.

**Federation of Master Builders.**
Gordon Fisher House,
14–15 Great James Street,
London, WC1N 3DP
Tel: 0171–242–7583
Fax: 0171–404–0296

The above runs a warranty scheme known as the National Register of Warranted Builders. Membership is available to *all* builders who meet its criteria. Members can provide their clients with an insurance backed warranty under-written by AXA Provincial. The cost is 1% of the gross contract price and each contract must individually be registered. The company can be contacted on 0171–404–4155 or in writing to the above address.

**Scottish Building Employers' Federation.**
Scottish Housebuilders Association,
Carron Grange,
Carron Grange Avenue,
Stenhousemuir, FK5 3BQ
Tel: 01324–555550

The Scottish Building Employers' Federation is the main employers' federation representing the building industry in Scotland. The Scottish Housebuilders Association covers mainly planning issues in the housebuilding sector.

## CAVITY WALL INSULATION AND DRAUGHT PROOFING

**National Cavity Insulation Association.**
**External Wall Insulation Association.**
**National Association of Loft Insulation Contractors.**
**Draught Proofing Advisory Association.**
**CEED (Council for Energy Efficiency Development).**
PO Box 12,
Haselmere,
Surrey, GU27 3AH
Tel: 01428–654011

All the above promote the good standards of their members, answer public enquiries, help mediate through the customer protection plan, and may also help consumers if a member firm ceases trading.

## COMPLAINTS AGAINST YOUR COUNCIL

Your local council will do its utmost to provide you with a fast and helpful response to your enquiries. They will often have their own internal complaints procedure, but if you are not satisfied you can contact the Local Government Ombudsman. Please contact the ombudsman for your area.

**Greater London, Kent and East Sussex**
Local Government Ombudsman.
21 Queen Anne's Gate,
London, SW1H 9BU
Tel: 0171–915–3210
Fax: 0171–233–0396

**East Anglia, Essex, Surrey, West Sussex, the south west, the south and most of central England (except Birmingham)**
Local Government Ombudsman.
The Oaks No 2,
Westwood Way,
Westwood Business Park,
Coventry, CV4 8JB
Tel: 01203–695999
Fax: 01203–695902

**Birmingham, Cheshire, Derbyshire, Nottinghamshire, Lincolnshire and the north of England**
Local Government Ombudsman.
Beverley House,
17 Shipton Road,
York, YO30 5FZ
Tel: 01904–663200
Fax: 01904–663269

**Scotland**
Local Government Ombudsmen.
23 Walker Street,
Edinburgh, EH3 7HX
Tel: 0131–225–5300
Fax: 0131–225–9495

**Wales**
Local Government Ombudsmen.
Derwen House,
Court Road,
Bridgend, F31 1BN
Tel: 01656–661325
Fax: 01656–658317

**Northern Ireland**
Local Government Ombudsmen.
33 Wellington Place,
Belfast, BT1 6HN.
Tel: 01232–233821
Fax: 01232–234912

You can also use the website at http://www.open.gov.uk/lgo

## CONSUMER HELP

**British Board of Agrément (BBA).**
PO Box 195,
Bucknalls Lane,
Garston,
Watford,
Hertfordshire, WD2 7NG
Tel: 01923–665300
Fax: 01923–666301
BBA Hotline: 01923–665400
Email: bba@btinternet.com
Website: http://www.bbacerts.co.uk

The above is a Government backed organisation with the following functions:

- To assess and test innovative construction products for safety, installation, durability criteria and issue Certificates which are reviewed normally every three years.

- To approve installers of certain systems e.g. injected cavity wall insulation and to monitor these regularly. It produces a 'Directory of Installers' and an 'Approved Products Guide'.

- Publications may be purchased direct from the BBA's Sales & Marketing Department or from its Monthly Datafile subscription scheme.

- Membership of the European Union of Agrément which aims to harmonise standards.

- Membership of the European Organisation for Technical Approvals, coordinating body for the issue of European Technical Approvals.

**Building Centre.**
26 Store Street,
London, WC1E 7BT
Tel: 0171–692–4000

The above contains a permanent exhibition of building materials and fittings on show to the public. The bookshop sells guides on home improvements and the ACA and JCT Minor Works contracts. The centre maintains an extensive reference library and free literature is available to members of the public. There is a free book catalogue and a mail order service. (Tel: 0171–637–3151).

**Companies House.**
Crown Way,
Maindy,
Cardiff, CF4 3UZ
Tel: 01222–388588

The above holds a register of companies, their registered office addresses, their directors and the trading status of each company.

**The Consumers Association.**
2 Marylebone Road,
London, NW1 4DF
FREEPHONE: 0800–252100 for subscription details.

The above provides the following:

- 'Which?' published monthly including DIY, energy saving, plumbing, heating systems, wiring, lighting and financial advice (often kept also in main branch libraries), and several bookshops.

- For an additional fee, subscribers can have access to a team of lawyers who will give telephone advice, take up a complaint on your behalf, and help you take a case through the County Court.

**Office of Fair Trading (OFT).**
PO Box 366,
Hayes,
UB3 1XB

Consumer Information Line: 0345–224499 for guidance on where to get practical help.

Publications Line: Tel: 0870–6060321
Fax: 0870–6070321
Email:
oft@echristain.co.uk

The aim of the OFT is to promote the economic interests of consumers by safeguarding effective competition, removing trading malpractices and publishing appropriate advice.

The above produces a number of free publications including:

- 'Home improvements'

- 'Your guide to personal finance'

- 'Using an estate agent to buy or sell your home'

- 'A Buyers Guide'

- 'A Guide to the Office of Fair Trading'

## CRAFTSMEN

**The Guild of Master Craftsmen Ltd.**
Castle Place,
166 High Street,
Lewes,
East Sussex, BN7 1XU
Tel: 01273–478449

The above aims to bring together all skilled people engaged in a craft, art, trade, profession or vocation in order to safeguard the interests of craftsmen and the public. It sets standards for membership, publicises the Guild through national and local media, promotes research and provides a helpline to assist the general public to find craftsmen. It also provides a conciliation service to help resolve disputes.

## DAMP-COURSE AND WOOD TREATMENT

**British Wood Preserving and Damp-proofing Association.**
Building No 6,
The Office Village,
Romford Road,
Stratford,
London, E15 4EA
Tel: 0181–519–2588
Fax: 0181–519–3444

The above is a trade organisation which keeps a list of members, provides training, technical advice and sometimes provides protection for a guarantee where a member company goes out of business (see top of next column).

**Guarantee Protection Trust Ltd.**
27 London, Road,
High Wycombe,
Buckinghamshire, HP11 1BW
Tel: 01494–447049

To protect consumers against a member firm going into liquidation, the Guarantee Protection Trust provides insurance backing to long term guarantees of dampproofing and timber treatment. There is a fee to pay on joining the scheme.

## DECORATORS

**British Decorators Association.**
32 Coton Road,
Nuneaton,
Warwickshire, CV11 5TW
Tel: 01203–353776

The above will act as arbitrator in the event of a complaint about a decorator's work, provided the individual is a member of the association.

## DOUBLE GLAZING

**British Plastics Federation.**
6 Bath Place,
Rivington Street,
London, EC2A 3JE
Tel: 0171–457–5000

The above is concerned with PVC surrounds to windows, not glazing. The federation also provides a plastic and rubber advisory service – Tel: 0991–908070.

**Glass and Glazing Federation (GGF).**
44–48 Borough High Street,
London, SE1 1XB
Tel: 0171–403–7177

The above keeps a list of members who work to a Code of Ethical Practice and has a conciliation service should a customer and a member company not see eye to eye over work carried out.

## ELDERLY

**Age Concern England.**
Astral House,
1268 London, Road,
London, SW16 4ER
Tel: 0181–679–8000
Fax: 0181–679–6069

**Age Concern Scotland.**
113 Rose Street,
Edinburgh, EH2 3DT
Tel: 0131–220–3345

**Age Concern Cymru.**
4th Floor,
1 Cathedral Road,
Cardiff, CF1 9SD
Tel: 01222–371566

**Age Concern Northern Ireland.**
3 Lower Crescent,
Belfast, BT7 1NR
Tel: 01232–245729

**Help the Aged.**
St James's Walk,
London, EC1R 0BE
Tel: 0171–253–0253

## ELECTRICAL CONTRACTORS

**The Electrical Contractors Association (ECA).**
ESCA House,
34 Palace Court,
London, W2 4HY
Tel: 0171–229–1266
Fax: 0171–221–7344
Email: electricalcontractors@eca.co.uk.
Website: http://www.eca.co.uk.

The above has some 2000 members on a register available from the ECA Membership Services Department. Its members work to relevant British Standards and a code of Fair Trading. Their work is backed by the ECA Warranty Scheme and Bond Scheme.

**SELECT.**
Bush House,
Bush Estate,
Midlothian, EH26 0SB
Tel: 0131–445–5577

Membership of SELECT guarantees a minimum standard of electrical work. Codes of practice and guarantee schemes protect the consumer.

**National Inspection Council for Electrical Installation Contracting (NICEIC).**
Vintage House,
37 Albert Embankment,
London, SE1 7UJ
Tel: 0171–582–7746

The above protects the consumer of electricity. It does this by maintaining a Roll of Approved Contractors who have been assessed by one of the Council's forty one inspecting engineers.

## EMPTY HOMES

**Empty Homes Agency Ltd (EHA).**
195–197 Victoria Street,
London, SW1E 5NE
Tel: 0171–828–6288
Fax: 0171–828–7006
Website://www.users.globalnet.co.uk/~eha/hotline.htm

The above is an independent housing charity working with local authorities, housing associations and the property professions to return empty property back into use. It can provide advice on letting your property and contacts with your local authority or appropriate housing associations. The EHA does not rent or own property.

Since November 1997, the EHA has successfully operated the London Empty Homes hotline (Tel: 0870 901–6303); an empty property reporting and action service involving the public, property owners and 32 London Boroughs. In October 1998, the EHA launched the National Approved Letting Scheme. The Scheme will be an accreditation membership scheme which aims to raise letting and management service standards provided by agents and housing associations within the private rented sector.

## ENERGY EFFICIENCY AND INSULATION

**Energy Action Grants Agency.**
Freepost PO Box 130,
Newcastle-Upon-Tyne, NE99 2RP

The above gives information about grants where thermal insulation and draught proofing are not adequate. These grants may be obtained either from your local council or from 'eaga' on behalf of the Home Energy Efficiency Scheme (HEES), which provides government help.

**Eaga – Home Energy Efficiency Scheme.**
Eldon Court,
Eldon Square,
Newcastle-Upon-Tyne, NE1 7HA
Tel: 0191–230–1830
Fax: 0191–230–1823

**Energy Efficiency Office.**
Department of Energy,
1 Palace Street,
London, SW1E 5HE

The above produces the following publications:

- 'Handy Hints to Save Energy in Your Home'.
- 'Energy in Your Home'.
- 'Insulating Your Home'.
- 'Heating Your Home'.

**National Energy Services.**
Rockingham Drive,
Linford Wood,
Milton Keynes, MK14 6EG
Tel: 01908–672787

The above produces the booklet 'Your New Home and the National Home Energy Rating', which also gives a list of local assessors for the National Home Energy Ratings.

## ESTATE AGENTS

**National Association of Estate Agents (NAEA).**
Arbon House,
21 Jury Street,
Warwick, CV34 4EH
Tel: 01926–496800

**The Ombudsman for Estate Agents (OEA).**
Beckett House,
4 Bridge Street,
Salisbury,
Wiltshire, SP1 2LX
Tel: 01722–333306
Fax: 01722–332296

The Office of Fair Trading (see address under **CONSUMER HELP**) has a statutory obligation under the Estate Agents Act 1979 to monitor the fitness of people engaged in estate agency work. It can investigate complaints and warn estate agents but it cannot become involved in individual cases.

## FINANCE

**The Financial Services Authority.**
25 The North Collonade,
Canary Wharf,
London, E14 5HS
Tel: 0171–676–1000
Website: http://www.fsa.gov.uk

The above provides a number of useful publications including the free guide 'How to spot the Investment Cowboys'. It also has a central register listing all firms which are authorised to give financial advice, tel: 0171–929–3652. If you encounter problems relating to financial matters you should complain first to the supplier. If this does not resolve problems, contact the relevant Ombudsman or Arbitration Scheme.

The Banking Ombudsman
– Tel 0171–404–9944 or 0345–660–902
The Building Societies Ombudsman
– Tel: 0171–931–0044
The Insurance Ombudsman
– Tel: 0171–928–7600 or 0845–600–6666
The Personal Insurance Arbitration Scheme and the Council of Mortgage Lenders (CML) Arbitration Scheme– Tel: 0171–837–4483
The Personal Investment Ombudsman
– Tel: 0171–216–0016
The Investment Ombudsman
– Tel: 0171–796–3065
The Pensions Ombudsman
– Tel: 0171–834–9144
The Occupational Pensions Regulatory Authority
– Tel: 01273–627610.

## FIRE SAFETY

**The Home Office Fire Safety Unit.**
Room 706,
Horseferry House,
Dean Ryle Street,
London, SW1P 2AW
Tel: 0171–217–8280

The Home Office Fire Safety Unit produces pamphlets in the 'Fire Safety in the Home' series:

- 'Wake Up! Get a smoke alarm'.

- 'Fire extinguishers for the home'.

- 'Fire safety in the home'. Also available in large print, braille and audio cassette.

- 'Electrical safety leads to fire safety'.

- 'Get out, get the Brigade out, stay out' – geared to 7–10 year olds.

- 'Francis the Firefly' a story book for 4–8 year olds.

- 'Fire safety in high rise flats'.

Note that local fire brigades can provide specific advice on particular properties if requested.

## FLOOD PREVENTION

**Environment Agency.**
Rio House,
Waterside Drive,
Aztec West,
Almondsbury,
Bristol, BS12 4UD
Tel: 01454–624400

## GAS INSTALLERS

**CORGI – The Council for Registered Gas Installers.**
1 Elmwood,
Chineham Business Park,
Crockford Lane,
Basingstoke,
Hants, RG24 8WG
Tel: 01256–372200

To find a registered installer in your area call 01256 372300 and have your postcode handy.

It is a legal requirement that anyone who works on gas fittings and appliances registers with CORGI, the National Watchdog for Gas Safety. CORGI's role is to protect the public from unsafe gas installations and to ensure gas work is carried out safely and competently by registered installers.

If you have a complaint about safety standards of gas work carried out by a CORGI registered installer or an unregistered installer, you should write to CORGI's Customer Services Department at the address above.

## GRANTS

The Department of the Environment, Transport and the Regions (see address under **STATUTORY**) produces the booklet 'Housing Renovation Grants' which is also available from your local council:

## HAZARDOUS SUBSTANCES

### ASBESTOS

The Department of the Environment, Transport and the Regions produces the leaflet 'Asbestos in Housing'.

Note the Health and Safety Executive (HSE) provides advice on asbestos via its helpline (see **HEALTH AND SAFETY**).

The National Society for Clean Air and Environmental Protection (see **AIR PURITY**) produces the leaflet 'Asbestos'.

### LEAD IN PAINT

**Paintmakers Association.**
British Coatings Federation Limited,
James House,
Bridge Street,
Leatherhead,
Surrey, KT22 7EP
Tel: 01372–360660
Fax: 01372–376069

The above produces a leaflet entitled 'How to remove Old Lead Paint safely, A Guide for Painters'.

### METHANE

If you experience any problems in respect of methane gas, you should contact the Environmental Health Department of your local council.

### RADON

**The National Radiological Protection Board.**
Chilton,
Didcot,
Oxon, OX11 0RQ
Tel: 01235–831600
Fax: 01235–822746

The above is an independent body, part funded by the Department of Health, which gives information on the occurrence of, and exposure to, radiation. It reviews all sources of exposure and provides advice and free literature. Householders living in localised areas with high radon measurements can telephone the radon freephone number on 0800–614529.

In the case of electromagnetic radiation (power lines, substations) and radiowaves (mobile phones and base stations) and all other radiation topics, information can be obtained by writing to the Information Office at the above address or by telephone on 01235–822742, fax number 01235–822746, email on -information@ nrpb.org.uk, or its website, which is constantly being updated, http://www.nrpb. org.uk

Single copies of the following are available free of charge:

- 'Radon: At-a-glance'

- 'Radon: Questions and Answers'

The Department of the Environment, Transport and the Regions (see address under **STATUTORY**) produces the following free leaflets:

- 'Radon – A Householder's Guide'.

- 'Radon – A Guide for Homebuyers and Sellers'.

- 'Radon – A Guide to reducing levels in your home'.

- 'Radon – You can test for it'.

## HEALTH AND SAFETY

**Health and Safety Executive (HSE) Information Centre.**
Broad Lane,
Sheffield, S3 7HQ
HSE Infoline: 0541–545500

The above gives advice on the application of The Construction (Health, Safety and Welfare) Regulations 1996 (CHSW Regulations) and The Construction (Design and Management) Regulations 1994 (CDM Regulations).

**HSE Books.**
PO Box 1999,
Sudbury,
Suffolk, CO10 6FS
Tel: 01787–881165
Fax: 01787–313995

The HSE also produces priced and free publications available by mail order from the above and which are also available from good booksellers.

## HISTORIC BUILDINGS

**English Heritage.**
Fortress House,
23 Savile Row,
London, W1X 1AB
Tel: 0171–973–3000 or 3250

The above has produced 'The English Heritage Register of Buildings at Risk 1998' and 'A New Strategy' which gives advice to owners and the public on how to save them.

**Historic Scotland.**
Longmore House,
Salisbury Place,
Edinburgh, EH9 1SH
Tel: 0131–668–8600

**Cadw/Welsh Historic Monuments.**
The Welsh Office,
Cathays Park,
Cardiff, CF1 3NQ
Tel: 01222–500200

The above give advice on work to historic or listed buildings, as indeed do your local authority planning department and the Department of the Environment.

**Save Britain's Heritage.**
77 Cowcross Street,
London, EC1M 6BP
Tel: 0171–253–3500
Fax: 0171–253–3400
Email: save@btinternet.com

The above champions the cause of decaying country houses, redundant churches, mills, warehouses, cottages, town halls, railway stations, hospitals, asylums and military buildings. It can also save such buildings from demolition and advise members of the public in their reuse. For further information or publication list contact the above.

**Department for Culture, Media and Sport.**
Library and Public Enquiry Unit
2–4 Cockspur Street,
London, SW1Y 5DH
Tel: 0171–211–6000

The above can be contacted to check if your property is on the register of historic/listed buildings or has been removed from it.

## HOME PURCHASE

**Council of Mortgage Lenders (CML).**
3 Savile Row,
London, W1X 1AF
Tel: 0171–437–0075
Tel: 0171–440–2255 Recorded message information request line for members of the public.

The above is the main representative body for mortgage lending institutions, keeps a directory of members and produces the following booklets:

- 'How to buy a home'.
- 'How to buy a home in Scotland'.
- 'Taxation and the Home Buyer'.

If you wish to buy a publication you should dial the switchboard and ask for Publications. There are also reference leaflets produced by the individual building societies.

Note: If you need to use a mortgage broker you can check whether they subscribe to the Mortgage Code by calling 01782–216300. This is a self-regulating code of practice which guarantees you fair advice and the right to complain if something goes wrong.

The Department of the Environment, Transport and the Regions (see address under **STATUTORY**) produces the free booklet 'Your Right to Buy Your Home', also available from your local council. It also produces the booklet entitled 'Thinking of buying a council flat'.

The Office of Fair Trading (see address under **CONSUMER RIGHTS**) produces the following leaflets:

- 'Your guide to personal finance' (which contains information on mortgages).
- 'Using an Estate Agent to buy or sell your home'.

## HOUSING ASSOCIATIONS

These can be contacted through your local authority, Housing Advice Centre or the Yellow Pages.

## HOUSING BENEFIT

Contact your local Department of Social Security, Benefit Office. These can be found through your local telephone directory.

## INSURANCE

**Association of British Insurers.**
51 Gresham Street,
London, EC2V 7HQ
Tel: 0171–600–3333

The above represents around 440 insurance companies and publishes a range of leaflets on various types of insurance including:

- 'Buildings Insurance for Home Owners 1998 Information Sheet'.
- 'Home Contents Insurance'.
- 'Buying Life Insurance'.

The Insurance Ombudsman Bureau (see **FINANCE**) is an independent organisation which can arbitrate in disputes between policy holders and insurance companies.

**Building Guarantee Scheme (UK) Ltd.**
143 Malone Road,
Belfast, BT9 6SU
Tel: 01232–661717

The above operates Buildsure, an insurance backed guarantee scheme offered to customers of builders who are registered with Buildsure. The scheme deals with defects, disputes and insolvency of the builder. If you wish to obtain a Buildsure registered builder you can telephone 0345 697781.

## LAND AND TITLE

**H.M. Land Registry Headquarters.**
General Enquiries,
Lincolns Inn Fields,
London, WC2A 3PH
Tel: 0171–917–8888
Fax: 0171–955–0110

The above is a Government agency responsible for registering title to land in England and Wales and for recording dealings once the land is registered. Not all land in England and Wales is yet registered although there are 16 million registered properties. The Land Registry Index Map indicates which properties are registered and upon application and payment of a fee, members of the public may obtain the name and address of the registered owner and/or will be provided with a copy of the register and/or with the title plan. Enquiries should be made to establish which of the District Land Registries applies to your local area.

## LANDSCAPING

**The British Association of Landscape Industries.**
Landscape House,
Henry Street,
Keighley,
West Yorkshire, BD21 3DR
Tel: 01535–606139

The above is the national body representing landscape contractors in the United Kingdom. It provides information and aims to protect standards.

## LEASEHOLD/RIGHT TO BUY

**Leasehold Advisory Service (LEASE).**
8 Maddox Street,
London, W1R 9PN
Tel: 0171–493–3116
Fax: 0171–493–4318

The above advises on rights to buy, lease extensions and any other aspects of residential leasehold property, for example service charges, repairs and forfeiture. They also can put you in touch with the regional leasehold valuation tribunals.

**The Housing Corporation.**
Publications Department,
149 Tottenham Court Road,
London, W1P 0BN
Tel: 017–393–2000

The above produces the 'Guide to the Right to Acquire' which allows eligible tenants of registered social landlords, such as Housing Associations, the right to buy the house they currently rent.

The Department of the Environment, Transport and the Regions (see address under **STATUTORY**) produces free booklets:

- 'Leasehold Houses. Your Right to Buy the Freehold of your House or Extend your Lease'.

- 'Leasehold Flats. Your Right to Buy the Freehold or Renew your Lease'.

- 'Leasehold Houses'

- 'Leasehold Flats'

- 'Right of First Refusal'

- 'Long Leaseholders. Your rights and responsibilities'.

## LEGAL

**Council for Licensed Conveyancers.**
16 Glebe Road,
Chelmsford,
Essex, CM1 1QG
Tel: 01245–349599

The above Council regulates, educates, disciplines licenced conveyancers who provide conveyancing services in competition with solicitors.

**The Law Society**.

The Society no longer provides a legal advice line to the public. However, 'The Solicitors Regional Directory' gives lists of solicitors by category of service and is obtainable from local libraries or local Citizens Advice Bureaux.

The Lord Chancellor's Department produces a leaflet entitled 'Small Claims at the County Court' which is available from your local County Court.

## LIGHT POLLUTION

**The Institute of Lighting Engineers.**
Lennox House,
9 Lawford Road,
Rugby,
Warwickshire, CV21 2DZ
Tel: 01788–576492
Fax: 01788–540145

The above produces the leaflet 'Guidance Notes for the reduction of light pollution'.

## MANAGING AND LETTING AGENTS

**Association of Residential Managing Agents (ARMA).**
P.O. Box 1863,
London, W10 4ZB
Tel: 0181–960–9077
Fax: 0181–960–9008

The above is the only professional body in England and Wales that focuses exclusively on block (multi-dwelling) management of residential property whether for landlords or residential management companies. Members comply with ARMA's Code of Practice and with the RICS Residential Management Code.

**Association of Residential Letting Agents (ARLA).**
Maple House,
53–55 Woodside Road,
Amersham,
Bucks, HP6 6AA
Tel: 01494–431680
Fax: 01494–431530

The above is the professional and regulatory body for letting agents. It provides guidelines, training, advice and can offer an arbitration service. The leaflet 'Trouble free letting' is available by sending a stamped addressed envelope.

## MORTGAGES

**Moneyfacts Publications.**
Moneyfacts House,
66–70 Thorpe Road,
Norwich,
Norfolk, NR1 1BJ
Tel: 01603–476476
Fax: 01603–476477

The above publishes 'Moneyfacts', the monthly guide to investment and mortgage rates.

**Charterhouse Communications Ltd.**
3rd Floor,
4–8 Tabernacle Street,
London, EC2A 4LU
Tel: 0171–638–1916

The above publish:

- 'What Mortgage?' a monthly magazine for consumers.

- 'Mortgage Finance Gazette' a monthly trade magazine aimed at banks, building societies, insurance companies, centralised mortgage lenders and anyone associated with the mortgage lending industry from solicitors to IT. (Editorial coverage includes news, loans, savings, technology, life and general insurance, title and creditor insurance, interest only, building society conversions, mergers and acquisitions, direct market, analysis on topical issues, legal issues, company profiles, in-depth features and special reports.)

- 'Building Societies Yearbook' the Official Handbook of the Building Societies Association. Published annually at the end of July. (It includes balance sheets of all leading building societies including directors and principal executives, major subsidiaries, lending policy; all the addresses of branches and agencies in the country, including ex-building societies; an historical listing of all mergers; BSA information including the annual report and details of BSA affiliated associations; statistics tables, building society league table; International Organisations; Directory of Surveyors.)

**Matching Hat Ltd.**
Penthouse Suite,
143 Charing Cross Road,
London, WC2H 0EE
Tel: 0171–478–4700

The above publish 'Your Mortgage?' magazine, monthly.

## NEIGHBOURHOOD WATCH

**National Neighbourhood Watch Association.**
Dixon House,
1 Lloyds Avenue,
London, EC3 3DH
Tel: 0171–680–9317

## NOISE POLLUTION

**The National Society for Clean Air and Environmental Protection (NSCA).**
136 North Street,
Brighton, BN1 1RG
Tel: 01273–326313

The above (see also under **AIR PURITY**) provides general information on dealing with noise and supplies the following leaflets:

- 'Noise Pollution'. (This gives an extensive list of the organisations you can complain to in relation to airports, military aircraft and railways.)

- 'Noise – How to keep the peace with your neighbours'.

**Mediation UK.**
82a Gloucester Road,
Bishopston,
Bristol, BS7 8BN
Tel: 0117–904–6661

The above provides details of local mediation services in respect of noise pollution. It also provides other mediation services including resolution of disputes between neighbours.

**The Noise Abatement Society.**
PO Box 518,
Eynsford,
Dartford,
Kent, DA4 0LL
Tel: 01695–725121

Building Research Establishment.
(see **STRUCTURAL SAFETY**)
The above provides advice on sound insulation.

Department of the Environment Transport and the Regions.
(see address of Free Literature Service of the DETR under **STATUTORY**)
The above produces the following booklets:

- 'Bothered by noise? What you can do about it'

- 'Constant barking can be avoided'

## ORDNANCE SURVEY

**Ordnance Survey.**
Romsey Road,
Southampton,
United Kingdom, SO16 4GU
Tel: 08456–050505 Customer Helpline.
Email: custinfo@ordsvy.gov.uk
Website: http://www.ordsvy.gov.uk

The above provides information on local agents for ordnance survey maps. Postal enquiries should be addressed to customer information.

## PLUMBING AND CENTRAL HEATING

**Institute of Plumbing.**
64 Station Lane,
Hornchurch,
Essex, RM12 6NB
Tel: 01708–472791
Fax: 01708–448987
Information line on internet – info@plumbers.org.uk

The above provides technical advice, produces free booklets, maintains standards of plumbing in the public interest and provides lists of local qualified professional plumbers.

**The Association of Plumbing & Heating Contractors (APHC).**
15 Ensign House,
Ensign Business Centre,
Westwood Way,
Coventry, CV4 8JA
Tel: 01203–470626
Fax: 01203–470942

The above operates in England and Wales and has a database of members who operate to a code of fair trading endorsed by the Office of Fair Trading. Their members are professionally trained and competent and carry full liability insurance of at least £1 million. A guarantee of work is offered and members give written quotations.

**Heating and Ventilating Contractors' Association (HVCA).**
ESCA House,
34 Palace Court,
London, W2 4JG
Tel: 0171–315–4900
Heating link line: 0345–581158 for information on members in relevant areas.

The above is the officially recognised organisation representing central heating contractors. It exists to promote fair dealing professional services and high installation standards. The HVCA Double Guarantee Scheme protects householders if an HVCA installer fails to fulfil his obligations. A directory of members can be purchased from the publications unit on 01768–864771.

**Scottish and Northern Ireland Plumbing Employers' Federation.**
2 Walker Street,
Edinburgh, EH3 7LB
Tel: 0131–225–2255
Fax: 0131–226–7638

The above is the national trade association for the Plumbing and Domestic Heating industry in Scotland and Northern Ireland. It provides a list of members, technical advice and operates a complaint procedure using their Code of Fair Trading and Guarantee of Work Schemes.

## RESIDENTS ASSOCIATIONS

**The Federation of Private Residents' Associations Ltd.**
62 Bayswater Road,
London, W2 3PS
Tel/Fax: 0171–402–1581

The above is the co-ordinating body for tenants'/residents' associations in blocks of flats throughout the UK. It deals with the following:

- Answers queries on maintenance of the block, legal advice, advice in disputes between landlords/managing agents and tenants and how to buy or extend the lease.

- Assists in the formation of residents' associations

- Makes representations to Government for improvements in housing legislation

- Produces an information pack and a quarterly newsletter

- Produce for sale the following booklets:
  – 'Running a block of leasehold flats'
  – 'Tenants' collective rights to buy the freehold and tenants individual rights to extend a lease'

– 'Participation agreement for collective enfranchisement'
– 'Summary of rights' (free to members)

## ROOFING CONTRACTORS

**National Federation of Roofing Contractors.**
24 Weymouth Street,
London, W1N 4LX
Tel: 0171–436–0387

The above represents contractors and manufacturers, provides technical information and operates a ten year Co-Partnership Guarantee.

**Mastic Asphalt Council.**
Claridge House
5 Elwick Road,
Ashford,
Kent, TN23 1PD
Tel: 01233–634411
Fax: 01233–634466

The above provides a free technical service and offers an insurance backed guarantee, which must be taken out before work starts, which safeguards clients if a contractor goes into liquidation.

## SECURITY

**Safe Neighbourhoods Unit (SNU).**
16 Winchester Walk,
London, SE1 9AG
Tel: 0171–403–6050

The above should only be contacted by local councils, managing agents and resident associations, not by individual members of the public, in order to obtain advice on security and community safety.

**The Home Office.**
Publicity Unit,
Room 155,
50 Queen Anne's Gate,
London, SW1H 9AT
Tel: 0171–273–2193

The above or the police can supply the following leaflets:

- 'Your Practical Guide to Crime Prevention'

- 'Beat the Burglar'

- 'Peace of Mind While You're Away'

The police can supply the following leaflets:

- 'Secured by Design' – this is used by architects and developers in the design of new housing.

- 'Get Your Own Back' – this deals with photographing valuable articles to enable the police to recover them if stolen. The free leaflet is available from your local library or from the nearest police station.

Note: The 'Bumblebee Property Bank' is a database of 'identifiable' pieces of property recovered by the police and is located at New Scotland Yard. For an appointment to view the images on the database, telephone 0171– 230–1970.

**The Master Locksmiths Association.**
Unit 4–5, Woodford Halse Business Park,
Woodford Halse,
Daventry,
Northants, NN11 6PZ
Tel: 01327–262255

The above will be able to advise you of an approved locksmith in your area.

## SELF BUILD

**Community Self-Build Agency.**
40 Bowling Green Lane,
London, EC1R 0NE
Tel: 0171–415–7092

The above promotes the idea of groups of people in housing need building their own home by pooling their resources. It provides independent advice, particularly for potential self builders. The agency encourages the sharing of good practice through its publications, regional events, training and the initiation of these schemes.

## SOLAR HEATING

**The Centre for Alternative Technology (CAT).**
Machynlleth,
Powys,
Wales, SY20 9AZ
Tel: 01654–702400

The above offers a free information service for brief enquiries or you can send a stamped addressed envelope. It also can sell you two booklets called 'Tapping the Sun. A Solar Water-Heating Guide' and 'Solar Water-Heating. A DIY Guide'.

## SPECIAL NEEDS

**Centre for Accessible Environments.**
Nutmeg House,
60 Gainsford Street,
London, SE1 2NY
Tel/Minicom: 0171–357–8182
Fax: 0171–357–8183

Email: cae@globalnet.co.uk
Website: http://www.cae.org.uk

The above is a registered charity and is the information and training body on the accessibility of the built environment for disabled people. The following are available:

- Information, library and register of members.

- Access audits of buildings and appraisals of plans.

- Training workshops and seminars.

- The journal 'Access by Design'.

- Information sheets such as 'Access Design Sheet: 1 Ramps'

- The book entitled 'Wheelchair Housing Design Guide' may be purchased and it deals with design matters helpful to the home owner, architects and builders.

**Royal National Institute for the Blind.**
224 Great Portland Street,
London, W1N 8AB
Tel: 0171–636–1153

**Royal National Institute for the Deaf.**
19/23 Featherstone Street,
London, EC1Y 8SL
Tel: 0171–296–8000

**Disabled Living Foundation.**
380–384 Harrow Road,
London, W9 2HU
Tel: 0171–289–6111
Helpline: 0870–603–9177

The above is a national charity providing practical up to date advice and information on many aspects of living with disability for disabled and elderly people and their carers as follows.

- Free advice is given to the general public through written correspondence.

- Publications can be purchased from the marketing department.

- Information is available on CD-ROM.

- Advice on equipment can be obtained and there is an equipment centre.

- There is a training programme.

## STANDARDS

**British Standards Institution.**
Sales Department,
Linford Wood,
Milton Keynes, MK14 6LE
Tel: 01908–220022

## STATUTORY

**Department of the Environment, Transport and the Regions (DETR).**
Eland House,
Bressenden Place,
London, SW1E 5DU
Tel: 0171–890–3000

Issues relevant to the Department of the Environment, Transport and the Regions, in respect of Northern Ireland, Scotland and Wales can be raised on the following telephone numbers:

Northern Ireland – 0171–210–3000
                   01232–520700
Scotland      – 0171–270–4744
                 0131–244–1111
Wales        – 0171–270–0566
                 01222–825111

**Department of the Environment, Transport and the Regions**
Free Literature Service,
PO Box 236,
Wetherby,
West Yorkshire, LS23 7NB
Tel: 0870–1226–236
Fax: 0870–1226–237

The DETR produces free booklets on planning and building regulations:

● 'Planning – A Guide for Householders'.

● 'Planning Permission – A Guide for Business'.

● 'Your Garden Walls – Better to be Safe …'

● 'A Householder's Planning Guide for the Installation of Satellite Television Dishes'.

● 'Protected Trees: a guide to tree preservation procedures'.

● 'Building Regulations Explanatory Booklet'.

● 'The Building Regulations and Fire Safety Procedural Guide'.

**Department of the Environment, Transport and the Regions.**
Publications Sales Centre.
Unit 21,
Goldthorpe Industrial Estate,
Goldthorpe,
Rotherham, S63 9BL
Tel: 01709–891318
Fax: 01709–881673

The DETR produces priced publications. See also telephone directory for addresses of local planning and building control departments for advice on planning permission, building regulations, and conservation areas.

## STRUCTURAL ENGINEERS

**The Institute of Structural Engineers.**
11 Upper Belgrave Street,
London, SW1X 8BH
Tel: 0171–235–4535

The above will provide information on chartered structural engineers in your area.

## STRUCTURAL SAFETY

**Building Research Establishment (BRE).**
Garston,
Watford,
Herts, WD2 7JR
Advisory Service Tel: 01923–664664
Email: enquiries@bre.co.uk

The above has published guidance on categories of structural defects in BRE Digest 251 entitled 'Assessment of damage in low rise buildings with particular reference to progressive foundation movement'.

It also produces information on many other subjects related to the home.

## TECHNICAL INFORMATION

**Construction Research Communications Limited.**
151 Rosebery Avenue,
London, EC1R 4QX
Tel: 0171–505–6622
Fax: 0171–505–6606
Email: crc@construct.emap.co.uk
Website: www.emap.com/construct/crc

The above is the publisher for the Building Research Establishment and other organisations which deal with home issues. A list of the many home related subjects is contained in the booklet 'Construction Publications 1997'.

## TREES

**Arboricultural Association.**
Ampfield House,
Ampfield,
Nr Romsey,
Hants, SO51 9PA
Tel: 01794–368717

Founded in 1964 the aims of the above are to conserve, enhance and protect Britain's heritage of amenity trees and it publishes the following two national directories which are updated each year.

● The Directory of Approved Contractors

● The Directory of Registered Consultants

There are three wings to the Associations membership, the Tree Officer, Contractor and Consultant. Householders should feel able to contact their local tree officer to discuss any tree related matter with an impartial professional.

## VALUATION AND RENT ASSESSMENT

**The Incorporated Society of Valuers and Auctioneers (ISVA).**
3 Cadogan Gate,
London, SW1X 0AS
Tel: 0171–235–2282

Leasehold Valuation Tribunals and Rent Assessment Panels:

London   Tel: 0171–446–7700
Merseyside & Cheshire   Tel: 0151–236–3521
Greater Manchester & Lancashire   Tel: 0161–832–9661
West Midlands   Tel: 0121–643–8336
Northern & Yorkshire   Tel: 0113–243–9744
East Midlands   Tel: 0115–947–3825
Chilterns, Thames & Eastern   Tel: 01223–505112
Southern & South Eastern   Tel: 01243–779394
South Western   Tel: 0117–929–9431
Wales   Tel: 01222–231687

## WARRANTY

**England**
National House-Building Council.
Buildmark House,
Chiltern Avenue,
Amersham,
Bucks, HP6 5AP
Tel: 01494–434477
Fax: 01494–735201

**Scotland**
National House-Building Council,
Scotland.
42 Colinton Road,
Edinburgh, EH10 5BT
Tel: 0131–313–1001

**Northern Ireland and Isle of Man**
National House-Building Council,
Northern Ireland.
Holyrood Court,
59 Malone Road,
Belfast, BT9 6SA
Tel: 01232–683131

The above provides the following:

- NHBC produces the publication 'Guide to your New Home' and a free video explaining warranty cover.

- It provides details of the Buildmark Warranty.

- It offers a free conciliation service if problems occur between you and your builder during the first two years of the Buildmark cover.

- Problems should initially be reported in writing to your builder during the first two years of Buildmark cover, thereafter they should be reported to your regional NHBC office.

- NHBC carries out spot inspections from time to time on properties registered under its Buildmark scheme to check that the builder is complying with NHBC Technical Standards.

## DISCLAIMER

Before commissioning work by a builder or a member of a specialist trade e.g. plumber, electrician, decorator, carpenter etc it is wise to ask for proof of their membership of a recognised trade association and the safeguards that this membership offers. Wherever possible we have given information about the relevant trade associations, their aims, standards and the services that they offer. We also state if there is a warranty scheme, who is responsible where failures in services occur and how to complain.